IXL MATH WORKBOOK

THE ULTIMATE
SEVENTH GRADE
MATH WORKBOOK

ISBN: 9781947569621
27 26 25 24 23 2 3 4 5 6
Printed in China

Table of Contents

Learn!

You can classify numbers in a few different ways.

Rational numbers are numbers that can be written as a quotient of two integers where the denominator is not zero. For example, you can write the rational number 0.25 as $\frac{1}{4}$.

Integers can be positive, negative, and zero, but they do not have fractional or decimal parts. Integers are rational numbers since you can write a number like -7 as $-\frac{7}{1}$.

Whole numbers include the counting numbers and zero. Whole numbers are also rational numbers since you can write a number like 18 as $\frac{18}{1}$.

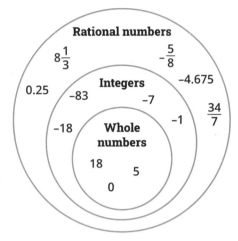

Write the most specific classification for each number. Remember to first simplify fractions, if possible.

-13 _____ integer _____

$\frac{3}{5}$ _____

0.567 _____

0 _____

$-\frac{21}{8}$ _____

51 _____

7.3 _____

-26 _____

$-16\frac{2}{3}$ _____

$\frac{36}{3}$ _____

9.78 _____

$-\frac{12}{4}$ _____

IXL.com skill ID

6KA

For more practice, visit IXL.com or the IXL mobile app and enter this code in the search bar.

Determine whether each statement is true or false.

4 is a rational number.	(True)	False
–81 is a whole number.	True	False
10 is an integer.	True	False
$\frac{16}{2}$ is a rational number.	True	False
$-\frac{1}{3}$ is an integer.	True	False
$8\frac{3}{4}$ is a rational number.	True	False
Both 99 and $\frac{13}{13}$ are rational numbers.	True	False
Both $-16\frac{2}{5}$ and –20 are integers.	True	False
0 is both an integer and a whole number.	True	False
A negative number is always an integer.	True	False
A whole number is a rational number.	True	False
A rational number can be written as a fraction.	True	False
An integer that is not negative is a whole number.	True	False

6 Terminating and repeating decimals

Learn!

You can use long division to write any rational number as a decimal, and the decimal will either terminate or repeat. A **terminating decimal** has a remainder of 0. A **repeating decimal** will repeat the same digit or digits without end. Look at the examples.

Write $\frac{3}{8}$ as a decimal.

```
    0.375
8) 3.000
  - 2 4
    60
  - 56
    40
  - 40
     0
```

The remainder is 0, so it is a **terminating decimal.**

Write $\frac{3}{11}$ as a decimal.

```
      0.2727
11) 3.0000
   - 2 2
     80
   - 77
     30
   - 22
     80
   - 77
      3
```

The digits 2 and 7 will repeat without end, so it is a **repeating decimal**. You can use a bar over those digits to show that they repeat.

So, $\frac{3}{8}$ written as a decimal is 0.375.

So, $\frac{3}{11}$ written as a decimal is $0.\overline{27}$.

Use long division to write each rational number as a decimal. Remember to write repeating decimals with a bar over any digits that repeat.

$\frac{3}{5}$ = _____

$-\frac{2}{9}$ = _____

$\frac{7}{8}$ = _____

Write each rational number as a terminating or repeating decimal.

$\dfrac{9}{12} =$ _____

$-\dfrac{17}{30} =$ _____

$\dfrac{11}{15} =$ _____

$\dfrac{4}{11} =$ _____

$2\dfrac{5}{8} =$ _____

$\dfrac{27}{40} =$ _____

$\dfrac{65}{12} =$ _____

$-3\dfrac{5}{18} =$ _____

$-\dfrac{37}{5} =$ _____

IXL.com
skill ID
M2D

Opposites and absolute value

Find the opposite of each number.

Opposite of 8 = __−8__   Opposite of −35 = _____   Opposite of 42 = _____

Opposite of $1\frac{1}{8}$ = _____   Opposite of $-\frac{3}{10}$ = _____   Opposite of −0.1 = _____

Find the absolute value of each number.

$|-26|$ = _____ $|73|$ = _____ $|-22|$ = _____ $|30|$ = _____

$-\left|-\frac{2}{15}\right|$ = _____ $|-7.1|$ = _____ $-|-1.9|$ = _____ $\left|-3\frac{2}{5}\right|$ = _____

Circle the greater number in each problem.

Opposite of −23	$|-26|$

Opposite of 2	$-|3|$

$\left|-\frac{7}{8}\right|$	Opposite of $-\frac{4}{5}$

$|-2.97|$	Opposite of 9.23

Opposite of 11.8	$-|12|$

Determine if the answer to each word problem is zero.

A hot-air balloon reached an elevation of 750 feet. Then, the balloon rose another 750 feet. How many feet above the ground was the balloon?　　　Zero　　　(Not zero)

Ella had –11 points after her first move in a board game. On the next move, she gained 11 points. What was her score after the second move?　　　Zero　　　Not zero

Jay earned $28.50 mowing his neighbor's lawn. The next day, he spent $28.50 on a new shirt. How much money does he have now?　　　Zero　　　Not zero

A dolphin was swimming 20 meters below sea level. After seeing a fish, the dolphin swam down 20 meters to catch it. At what depth did the dolphin catch the fish?　　　Zero　　　Not zero

When Adam went snowboarding, the temperature was –6.8°F. This was 6.8°F warmer than the average temperature for the month. What was the average temperature?　　　Zero　　　Not zero

---

Write your own word problem where the answer is zero.

_____

_____

_____

_____

IXL.com
skill ID
7SP

Learn!

You can use a number line to add integers. Start at the first addend. The second addend tells you how many units to move. Move right to add a positive number or left to add a negative number. The number you land on is the sum.

–7 + 9 = 2

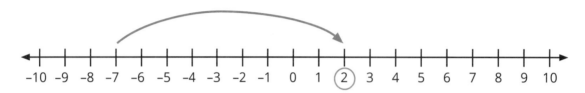

Use the number lines to add the integers.

$6 + (-1) = \underline{5}$

$-2 + 6 = \underline{}$

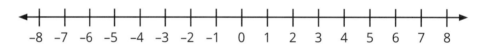

$-8 + 5 = \underline{}$

$-2 + (-4) = \underline{}$

$3 + (-8) = \underline{}$

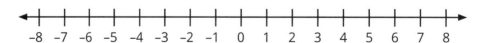

IXL.com
skill ID
A63

Learn!

You can also add integers using rules.

To add integers with the **same** sign, add the absolute value of each number.

The answer will have the same sign as the original numbers.

$$13 + 21 = 34$$

$$-13 + (-21) = -34$$

To add integers with **different** signs, subtract the absolute values of the numbers.

Keep the sign of the number with the larger absolute value.

$$-12 + 16 = 4$$

$$12 + (-16) = -4$$

Add the integers.

$-34 + (-25) =$ ___−59___ $-50 + 40 =$ _____ $-6 + 71 =$ _____

$-21 + (-34) =$ _____ $-3 + 30 =$ _____ $4 + (-14) =$ _____

$10 + (-22) =$ _____ $-8 + (-22) =$ _____ $-4 + (-67) =$ _____

$28 + (-15) =$ _____ $-84 + (-5) =$ _____ $68 + (-72) =$ _____

$99 + (-45) =$ _____ $-63 + 58 =$ _____ $54 + (-18) =$ _____

IXL.com
skill ID

QFU

Learn!

You can use a number line to subtract integers, too. Subtracting a number is the same as **adding the opposite**. So, you can change a subtraction problem into an addition problem. Then follow the same steps you would use to add integers using a number line.

$$-5 - 3 \longrightarrow -5 + (-3) = -8$$

Use the number lines to subtract. Remember to first change the subtraction problem into an addition problem.

$6 - (-1) = \underline{\quad 7 \quad}$
$\quad 6 + 1$

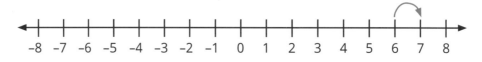

$-5 - 1 = \underline{\qquad}$

$-2 - (-7) = \underline{\qquad}$

$6 - 8 = \underline{\qquad}$

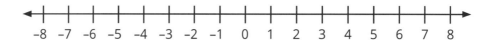

$-3 - (-3) = \underline{\qquad}$

IXL.com
skill ID
FGG

Learn!

You can also subtract integers using rules. Start by changing the subtraction problem into an addition problem. Then use the same rules that you would use to add integers.

–12 – 16 ⟶ –12 + (–16)
–12 + (–16) = –28

13 – 21 ⟶ 13 + (–21)
13 + (–21) = –8

15 – (–27) ⟶ 15 + 27
15 + 27 = 42

–25 – (–6) ⟶ –25 + 6
–25 + 6 = –19

Subtract the integers.

–21 – (–19) = __–2__
    –21 + 19

–3 – 25 = _____

11 – 21 = _____

–18 – 4 = _____

–9 – (–8) = _____

–30 – 20 = _____

–24 – 22 = _____

20 – (–45) = _____

48 – 75 = _____

37 – (–38) = _____

–44 – (–5) = _____

82 – (–5) = _____

17 – (–13) = _____

–8 – (–88) = _____

10 – 77 = _____

IXL.com
skill ID
HEU

Add or subtract the integers.

–9 + 4 = _____

8 – (–3) = _____

12 + (–5) = _____

–10 – 6 = _____

5 – 17 = _____

15 – (–13) = _____

–19 + (–32) = _____

–27 – (–3) = _____

16 + (–18) = _____

10 + (–70) = _____

–23 + 41 = _____

–72 – 28 = _____

18 – (–23) = _____

–14 – (–33) = _____

–34 + 58 = _____

–11 + (–66) = _____

–67 + (–9) = _____

62 – 84 = _____

–26 + 12 = _____

–91 – 40 = _____

72 + (–59) = _____

–32 – (–16) = _____

–89 + 25 = _____

39 – 75 = _____

Complete each puzzle.

Puzzle 1:
-2 → (+ 10) → 8
8 ↓ (- 9) → -1
-1 ← (+ 10) → 9
9 ↑ (- 11) → -2

Puzzle 2:
7 → (- 22) →
↓ (+ 10)
← (- 18)
↑

Puzzle 3:
80 → (- 75) →
↓ (- 8)
← (- 7)
↑

Puzzle 4:
→ (+ 8) →
↓ (+ 31)
6 ← (- 32)
↑

Puzzle 5:
→ (- 57) →
↓
1 ← (- 13)
↑ (+ 21)

Puzzle 6:
→ -43
↓ (+ 15)
← (+ 8)
↑ (- 7)

You can use the same rules as before to add or subtract positive and negative rational numbers. Try it! Add or subtract.

5.3 + (−2.7) = __2.6__   −11.7 − 0.8 = _____   3.4 + (−1.7) = _____

−6.2 − (−2.5) = _____   −7.2 + (−4.9) = _____   −0.2 − (−0.3) = _____

−9.7 + 14.2 = _____   16.8 − 19.5 = _____   −10.9 + (−1.1) = _____

−16.7 + (−2.4) = _____   −9.7 − (−8.8) = _____   8.51 − (−6.56) = _____

2.75 + (−2.75) = _____   8.55 + (−3.71) = _____   −5.52 − 11.28 = _____

−4.167 + 5.342 = _____   −0.713 − 5.311 = _____

IXL.com
skill ID
WCZ

Add or subtract.

$\dfrac{2}{7} + \left(-\dfrac{5}{7}\right) = \underline{-\dfrac{3}{7}}$

$-\dfrac{1}{5} - \dfrac{3}{5} = \underline{\hspace{2cm}}$

$-\dfrac{4}{9} + \dfrac{2}{3} = \underline{\hspace{2cm}}$

$\dfrac{3}{4} - \dfrac{11}{12} = \underline{\hspace{2cm}}$

$3\dfrac{2}{9} - \left(-\dfrac{5}{9}\right) = \underline{\hspace{2cm}}$

$3\dfrac{2}{3} - \left(-5\dfrac{2}{3}\right) = \underline{\hspace{2cm}}$

$-5\dfrac{1}{12} - \dfrac{1}{4} = \underline{\hspace{2cm}}$

$-2\dfrac{1}{2} + \left(-\dfrac{5}{8}\right) = \underline{\hspace{2cm}}$

$3 - \dfrac{5}{16} = \underline{\hspace{2cm}}$

$-\dfrac{17}{20} + 5 = \underline{\hspace{2cm}}$

$7\dfrac{3}{5} + \left(-6\dfrac{3}{10}\right) = \underline{\hspace{2cm}}$

$-2\dfrac{3}{20} - \left(-5\dfrac{2}{5}\right) = \underline{\hspace{2cm}}$

$-\dfrac{3}{5} + 6\dfrac{2}{3} = \underline{\hspace{2cm}}$

$\dfrac{4}{5} - \left(-\dfrac{5}{8}\right) = \underline{\hspace{2cm}}$

$-1\dfrac{1}{3} + 5\dfrac{11}{12} = \underline{\hspace{2cm}}$

$-\dfrac{9}{16} - 4\dfrac{3}{4} = \underline{\hspace{2cm}}$

$-7\dfrac{3}{8} + \dfrac{5}{6} = \underline{\hspace{2cm}}$

IXL.com
skill ID
SD2

Find the path from start to finish. Step only on spaces that have answers between –5 and 5. No diagonal moves are allowed.

START

$-\dfrac{2}{5} - \left(-\dfrac{9}{25}\right)$	$-2.7 + 8.6$	$8\dfrac{1}{20} - \left(-6\dfrac{3}{4}\right)$
$-5.3 - (-7.1)$	$-\dfrac{5}{8} + \left(-\dfrac{9}{16}\right)$	$3\dfrac{5}{6} + \left(-1\dfrac{2}{3}\right)$
$-9.17 - 6$	$5.95 - 11.36$	$-2\dfrac{4}{5} - \left(-2\dfrac{1}{2}\right)$
$5\dfrac{1}{2} - 11\dfrac{1}{2}$	$2.76 + (-2.76)$	$-0.9 + (-0.1)$
$4\dfrac{7}{10} + \left(-\dfrac{5}{6}\right)$	$-1.81 - (-6)$	$-5 + \left(-\dfrac{7}{8}\right)$
$-4.3 + 1.35$	$5.82 - (-3.5)$	$12\dfrac{5}{6} + \left(-5\dfrac{1}{4}\right)$

FINISH

Add or subtract. To help, first rewrite the problem so that the numbers have the same form.

$2.5 + 5\frac{1}{4} =$ _____

$-\frac{7}{10} + (-4.9) =$ _____

$-6\frac{1}{5} - (-1.5) =$ _____

$-8\frac{2}{5} + 8.65 =$ _____

$-9\frac{7}{10} + 4.2 =$ _____

$\frac{3}{20} - 0.5 =$ _____

$-5\frac{1}{2} - 11.28 =$ _____

$4\frac{3}{4} + (-2.03) =$ _____

$2.45 + \left(-\frac{4}{50}\right) =$ _____

$-1\frac{11}{25} + (-6.1) =$ _____

$-16.4 - \frac{1}{4} =$ _____

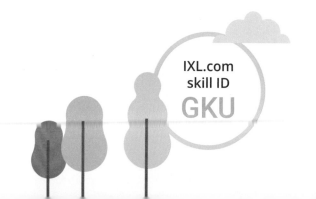

IXL.com
skill ID
GKU

Answer each question.

Anthony's family is playing a trivia game where points are added for correct answers and subtracted for incorrect answers. Anthony's score was –30 points before he earned 15 points for a correct answer. How many points does Anthony have after the correct answer?

_____

A brown pelican was flying at a height of 22 feet above the surface of the water. It dove 28 feet to catch a fish swimming underwater. What was the position of the fish compared to the surface of the water?

_____

Before running an experiment, Julie had 16.2 milliliters of liquid in a beaker. After the experiment, there was a change of –3.5 milliliters of liquid. How much liquid was left in Julie's beaker?

_____

Shawn borrowed $12.50 from his sister and wanted to pay her back. He then earned $40 babysitting. How much money will Shawn have after paying his sister back?

_____

The lowest temperature on record for Primrose Park is –15.7°F. The park's highest recorded temperature is 95.5°F warmer than the lowest temperature. What is the park's highest recorded temperature?

_____

Learn!

You can multiply and divide integers using rules. Look at the rules below.

When you multiply or divide two integers with the **same sign**, the answer will be **positive**.

$$3 \times 6 = 18 \qquad -5 \times (-4) = 20$$
$$24 \div 8 = 3 \qquad -14 \div (-2) = 7$$

When you multiply or divide two integers with **different signs**, the answer will be **negative**.

$$-9 \times 3 = -27 \qquad 4 \times (-7) = -28$$
$$-36 \div 6 = -6 \qquad 10 \div (-5) = -2$$

Multiply or divide.

$3 \times (-5) = \underline{-15}$ $-10 \times (-4) = \underline{}$ $-42 \div 7 = \underline{}$

$-64 \div (-8) = \underline{}$ $-7 \times (-4) = \underline{}$ $18 \div (-2) = \underline{}$

$-5 \times 12 = \underline{}$ $-6 \times (-6) = \underline{}$ $-88 \div 8 = \underline{}$

$-100 \div 10 = \underline{}$ $8 \times (-20) = \underline{}$ $-75 \div (-25) = \underline{}$

$-90 \div 3 = \underline{}$ $56 \div 4 = \underline{}$ $-4 \times 60 = \underline{}$

$30 \times (-7) = \underline{}$ $20 \times 11 = \underline{}$

IXL.com
skill ID
DQT

22 Multiplying and dividing integers

Keep going! Multiply or divide.

$-6 \times (-10) =$ ______ $-7 \times (-7) =$ ______ $5 \times (-70) =$ ______

$-48 \div (-8) =$ ______ $-40 \times (-3) =$ ______ $180 \div (-60) =$ ______

$-12 \times 8 =$ ______ $360 \div 9 =$ ______ $-50 \times (-8) =$ ______

$-200 \div 50 =$ ______ $8 \times (-4) =$ ______ $-45 \div 5 =$ ______

$-12 \times (-60) =$ ______ $150 \div (-30) =$ ______ $-40 \times 7 =$ ______

$-210 \div 3 =$ ______ $-6 \times 30 =$ ______ $-36 \div (-18) =$ ______

$12 \times 11 =$ ______ $-84 \div (-12) =$ ______ $15 \times (-9) =$ ______

$51 \div (-17) =$ ______ $-96 \div 24 =$ ______ $48 \div (-16) =$ ______

IXL.com
skill ID
R8D

Multiplying and dividing rational numbers

You can use the same rules as before to multiply or divide positive and negative rational numbers. Try it! Multiply or divide.

$-3.1 \times (-0.2) =$ 0.62

$-8.6 \times (-10) =$ ______

$2.67 \div (-0.3) =$ ______

$4.5 \div 0.6 =$ ______

$-0.78 \div 0.02 =$ ______

$6.3 \times (-2.4) =$ ______

$1.2 \times (-8.1) =$ ______

$10.23 \div (-1.1) =$ ______

$-8.9 \times (-0.35) =$ ______

$-60.5 \div 2.5 =$ ______

IXL.com
skill ID
K7V

Multiply or divide.

$$\frac{3}{8} \times \left(-\frac{1}{5}\right) = \underline{-\frac{3}{40}}$$

$$-\frac{3}{5} \div \frac{4}{5} = \underline{\hspace{2cm}}$$

$$\frac{5}{6} \div \left(-\frac{5}{12}\right) = \underline{\hspace{2cm}}$$

$$-1\frac{1}{7} \times \left(-\frac{1}{3}\right) = \underline{\hspace{2cm}}$$

$$3\frac{3}{8} \div \frac{1}{2} = \underline{\hspace{2cm}}$$

$$-2\frac{1}{2} \times \left(-\frac{8}{9}\right) = \underline{\hspace{2cm}}$$

$$\frac{2}{7} \times \left(-2\frac{5}{8}\right) = \underline{\hspace{2cm}}$$

$$-\frac{7}{9} \div \left(-3\frac{1}{9}\right) = \underline{\hspace{2cm}}$$

$$-1\frac{1}{6} \div 5\frac{1}{4} = \underline{\hspace{2cm}}$$

$$-1\frac{1}{3} \times 5\frac{1}{2} = \underline{\hspace{2cm}}$$

Draw a line between problems that have equivalent answers.

$-\dfrac{8}{15} \div \dfrac{4}{5}$

$\dfrac{1}{5} \div \left(-\dfrac{4}{3}\right)$

$14.4 \div (-1.2)$

$-\dfrac{1}{3} \div \dfrac{1}{2}$

$0.35 \div 7$

$2.5 \times (-0.5)$

$0.5 \times (-0.3)$

$-\dfrac{2}{5} \times \left(-\dfrac{1}{8}\right)$

$-\dfrac{7}{8} \times \left(-\dfrac{4}{3}\right)$

-2.5×4.8

$-\dfrac{3}{2} \times \dfrac{5}{6}$

$3.5 \div 3$

Multiply or divide. To help, first rewrite the problem so that the numbers have the same form.

$-3\frac{1}{4} \times (-0.4) =$ _____

$-2.25 \div \frac{1}{2} =$ _____

$0.75 \times \frac{3}{5} =$ _____

$-3.45 \div \left(-\frac{3}{10}\right) =$ _____

$-7.4 \times 1\frac{1}{2} =$ _____

$1\frac{1}{4} \times (-8.2) =$ _____

$-3.6 \div \left(-\frac{1}{4}\right) =$ _____

$-11.12 \div \left(-\frac{4}{5}\right) =$ _____

$22.96 \div \left(-\frac{2}{5}\right) =$ _____

IXL.com
skill ID
BXW

Multiply or divide. Use your answers to draw a path from start to finish.

START

| $-1\frac{3}{5} \times 2\frac{3}{8}$ | 3.8 | $9.36 \div (-2.4)$ | −3.9 | $-6.8 \times \left(-\frac{1}{2}\right)$ | 3.2 | $2\frac{1}{5} \times \left(-1\frac{1}{2}\right)$ |

$-2\frac{9}{40}$ $-3\frac{4}{5}$ 3.5   −3.3   3.4 $-3\frac{1}{10}$ $-3\frac{2}{5}$

| $-2\frac{1}{6} \div \frac{2}{3}$ | −1.9 | $-2.8 \div \left(-\frac{4}{5}\right)$ | −3.5 | $2.1 \times (-1.5)$ | −3.15 | $-6\frac{1}{4} \div 1\frac{7}{8}$ |

$3\frac{1}{4}$ −3.2   2.3   −2.5 $-3\frac{1}{5}$ $-3\frac{1}{3}$ $-7\frac{1}{7}$

| $9\frac{3}{5} \div 3\frac{1}{5}$ | −3 | $-1\frac{2}{5} \times 1\frac{2}{3}$ | −7.6 | $-1.52 \div \frac{1}{5}$ | −7.3 | -10.3×0.7 |

$3\frac{1}{5}$ $3\frac{5}{36}$ $-2\frac{1}{3}$ −3.04   −7.4   −7.7   −11

| $1\frac{1}{5} \times \left(-3\frac{1}{3}\right)$ | 4 | FINISH | 12 | $-2\frac{1}{5} \times \left(-5\frac{1}{2}\right)$ | −10 | $-11.1 \div 1.1$ |

Answer each question.

A hot-air balloon descends 1,200 feet in 4 minutes. What number represents the change in altitude in feet per minute?

$$-1{,}200 \div 4 = -300$$

Liz turned off the oven after baking cookies. The oven temperature then decreased at a rate of 37°F per minute. What number represents the change in temperature after 5 minutes?

_____

Chloe's basketball team scored 84 points in their last 3 games. What number represents the average number of points scored per game?

_____

Ed has $5\frac{1}{4}$ cups of flour to split equally among 3 cakes. What number represents the number of cups of flour per cake?

_____

The swimming pool at Camp Green Trails is emptied at the end of the summer for repairs. It takes 30 minutes for 486 liters of water to drain from the pool. What number represents the change in water in liters per minute?

_____

A diver descends at a rate of −18.2 feet per minute. From the surface of the water, the descent takes 3 minutes. What number represents the diver's final position, in feet, relative to the water's surface?

_____

Time for review! Add, subtract, multiply, or divide.

$-3 + 5 =$ _____

$-35 \div 7 =$ _____

$2 \times (-9) =$ _____

$4 - (-13) =$ _____

$-41 + (-33) =$ _____

$-18 - 25 =$ _____

$-11 \times 5 =$ _____

$-8 \times (-3) =$ _____

$30 + (-21) =$ _____

$-20 - (-50) =$ _____

$6 \times (-7) =$ _____

$-16 \div 4 =$ _____

$67 + (-46) =$ _____

$99 - (-30) =$ _____

$-7 \times 9 =$ _____

$-36 \div (-18) =$ _____

$-22 - (-16) =$ _____

$64 \div (-8) =$ _____

$36 + (-38) =$ _____

$360 \div (-9) =$ _____

$-51 \div 3 =$ _____

$51 + (-17) =$ _____

$-112 - 29 =$ _____

In each problem below, a student tried to solve a word problem but made an error. Identify the error in each student's work and correctly solve the word problem.

An excavator begins digging a hole for a new pool. If the excavator digs at a rate of 2 feet per hour, how deep will the hole be after 4 hours?

Diego's work:

$4 ÷ (−2) = −2$ The hole will be 2 feet deep.

What error did Diego make?	Show the correct work.

A catfish was swimming 5 feet below the surface of a lake. It swam down another 2 feet to avoid a boat floating on the surface. What is the position of the catfish compared to the surface of the lake?

Joy's work:

$−5 − 2 = −3$ The catfish is 3 feet below the surface.

What error did Joy make?	Show the correct work.

IXL.com
skill ID
2DD

Rational number operations

Add, subtract, multiply, or divide.

$-3.4 + 5.8 =$ _____

$-6\frac{2}{3} - \left(-1\frac{1}{2}\right) =$ _____

$2.3 \times (-7) =$ _____

$-\frac{3}{7} \times \frac{7}{12} =$ _____

$-1.7 + (-4.8) =$ _____

$-9.4 - 3.4 =$ _____

$-3\frac{1}{4} \div \frac{1}{2} =$ _____

$7.2 \div (-0.8) =$ _____

$-6\frac{3}{8} - 7\frac{3}{4} =$ _____

$-4.2 \div 1.2 =$ _____

$-1\frac{1}{4} \times 4\frac{1}{2} =$ _____

$12 \div \left(-\frac{2}{9}\right) =$ _____

$\frac{3}{8} + \left(-\frac{5}{12}\right) =$ _____

$7.5 - (-0.45) =$ _____

$-1\frac{1}{3} \times 6\frac{3}{5} =$ _____

$-3.5 \div (-0.14) =$ _____

$-8\frac{3}{4} + 10\frac{5}{6} =$ _____

$-17.51 + 3.93 =$ _____

Solve each problem. Remember to first rewrite the problem so that the numbers have the same form.

$-7.6 + 5\frac{2}{5} =$ _____

$-5.1 \div \left(-\frac{1}{20}\right) =$ _____

$1.7 \times \left(-\frac{3}{10}\right) =$ _____

$-6.4 \div \frac{1}{5} =$ _____

$-3\frac{1}{2} + (-3.8) =$ _____

$3\frac{4}{5} - (-1.8) =$ _____

$4.8 \times \left(-8\frac{2}{5}\right) =$ _____

$-5.7 \div \frac{3}{10} =$ _____

$2\frac{3}{25} + (-2.12) =$ _____

$-\frac{23}{50} - (-3.5) =$ _____

$-6\frac{27}{50} - 9.12 =$ _____

$-2.7 \times 5\frac{7}{20} =$ _____

CHALLENGE ZONE

Solve each problem. Remember to follow the order of operations.

$3 - 8.04 \div (-2) =$ ___7.02___

$3 - (-4.02) = 7.02$

$2\frac{1}{2} \times \left(-\frac{2}{3}\right) + \frac{2}{9} =$ _____

$-100 \div 3\frac{1}{3} \times 1\frac{5}{6} =$ _____

$-10.83 \div 0.2 - 1.03 =$ _____

$1.06 \div 0.5 + (-6.3) \times 0.3 =$ _____

$-7\frac{1}{2} \div \frac{5}{6} - \left(-8\frac{3}{7}\right) + 4\frac{4}{7} =$ _____

$1.8 - 2.2 \times 0.6 \div 0.3 =$ _____

Find the unit rate.

72 flowers in 9 vases   _____ flowers per vase

5 shelves hold 60 books   _____ books per shelf

25 apartments have 100 windows   _____ windows per apartment

2 hours to drive 136 miles   _____ miles per hour

80 pencils in 5 packs   _____ pencils per pack

9 lawns mowed in 6 hours   _____ lawns per hour

168 players on 12 teams   _____ players per team

18 gallons of water in 8 fish tanks   _____ gallons per fish tank

198 carrots in 22 bags   _____ carrots per bag

136 chairs at 17 tables   _____ chairs per table

5 minutes to swim 10 laps   _____ minutes per lap

18 dressers have 108 drawers   _____ drawers per dresser

184 socks in 46 packages   _____ socks per package

Unit prices

Find the unit price.

$7.98 for 2 bags of pretzels $ ________ per bag

$24.25 for 5 gallons of gas $ ________ per gallon

8-pack of batteries for $7.60 $ ________ per battery

4 T-shirts for $51 $ ________ per T-shirt

$10.50 for 14 sponges $ ________ per sponge

1.2 pounds of zucchini for $1.74 $ ________ per pound

$40 for a pack of 16 tickets $ ________ per ticket

$8.50 for 2.5 square feet of fabric $ ________ per square foot

Circle the better buy.

8 protein bars for $11.84	$7.60 for 5 protein bars
$8.40 for 20 paintbrushes	$1.68 for 7 paintbrushes
7 boxes of dog treats for $28.98	$32.48 for 8 boxes of dog treats
$1.44 for 16 ounces of apple juice	$1.32 for 12 ounces of apple juice

IXL.com skill ID N7G

Find the unit rate.

2 glasses hold $\frac{1}{2}$ of a liter of water

_____ liters per glass

$\frac{1}{4}$ of a cup of flour for every 3 teaspoons of sugar

_____ cups per teaspoon

$\frac{2}{3}$ of a cup of soap in 4 gallons of water

_____ cups per gallon

$\frac{1}{4}$ of a room painted every $\frac{1}{2}$ of an hour

_____ hours per room

$\frac{3}{4}$ of a stick of butter for $\frac{1}{3}$ of a batch of muffins

_____ sticks per batch

$\frac{1}{2}$ of an hour to walk $\frac{7}{8}$ of a mile

_____ miles per hour

$\frac{1}{10}$ of a pot holds $\frac{1}{5}$ of a pound of soil

_____ pounds per pot

$\frac{1}{4}$ of a tub of icing for $\frac{1}{3}$ of a dozen cupcakes

_____ tubs per dozen

Answer each question.

On the path in his neighborhood, Sam biked 4 miles in $\frac{2}{3}$ of an hour. At this rate, how far can Sam bike per hour?

_____

Josiah works at Bubbles & Sparkles Car Wash. He earned $15 after washing one car, and it took him $\frac{3}{4}$ of an hour. What is Josiah's hourly rate?

_____

Rory is making a big batch of soup. She uses $\frac{1}{8}$ of an onion for every $\frac{1}{4}$ of a cup of chicken broth. How much onion does she need for each cup of chicken broth?

_____

Jet is training for a 25-meter sprint. So far, his best time is $6\frac{1}{4}$ seconds. What is Jet's speed in meters per second?

_____

The most popular smoothie at Smoothie City uses $1\frac{1}{2}$ cups of spinach for every $\frac{3}{4}$ of a cup of mango. How much spinach is used per cup of mango?

_____

Mae is growing sunflowers in the community garden. She reads that the average sunflower grows $\frac{4}{5}$ of a foot every $\frac{1}{4}$ of a month. How many feet can Mae expect a sunflower to grow each month?

_____

IXL.com
skill ID
57X

Equivalent ratios

Fill in the missing number to complete each equivalent ratio.

4:5 = 16: __20__   3:4 = _____ :32   5:3 = 30: _____

32:6 = _____ :3   6:7 = 36: _____   8:5 = _____ :10

7:3 = _____ :15   14:21 = _____ :3   36:9 = 4: _____

3:8 = _____ :24   5:7 = 35: _____   12:20 = 3: _____

50:46 = 25: _____   35:50 = _____ :10   42:7 = 6: _____

45:25 = 9: _____   18:27 = _____ :3 $3:7 = 1\frac{1}{2}:$ _____

4.5:5.5 = _____ :1.1   17:13 = 34: _____ $4\frac{3}{5}:8 =$ _____ :16

16:13 = 48: _____ $37:23 = 12\frac{1}{3}:$ _____   4:5 = _____ :7.5

Learn!

When two ratios are equivalent, they can form a proportion. To determine if two ratios are equivalent, write them as fractions with a common denominator. Look at some examples.

1:5 and 2:10

$$\frac{1 \times 2}{5 \times 2} = \frac{2}{10}$$

$\frac{1}{5}$ and $\frac{2}{10}$ are equivalent, so the ratios form the proportion $\frac{1}{5} = \frac{2}{10}$.

6:8 and 3:12

$$\frac{6 \div 2}{8 \div 2} = \frac{3}{4} \qquad \frac{3 \div 3}{12 \div 3} = \frac{1}{4}$$

$\frac{3}{4}$ and $\frac{1}{4}$ are **not** equivalent, so the ratios do not form a proportion.

Circle each pair of ratios that forms a proportion.

(6:8 and 3:4)   15:18 and 5:6   3:7 and 9:21

28:8 and 14:4   3:7 and 18:35   9:6 and 36:24

6:15 and 12:25   16:10 and 48:30   32:42 and 16:22

15:20 and 6:8   16:24 and 14:21   3.5:4.5 and 8:9

$\frac{12}{5}$:3 and 13:15   1.6:8 and 0.8:4

IXL.com
skill ID
MJQ

Learn!

To solve a proportion, you can use inverse operations. Look at the example.

$$\frac{2}{15} = \frac{x}{45}$$

$$\frac{2}{15}(15 \cdot 45) = \frac{x}{45}(15 \cdot 45)$$ First, get rid of the denominators. Multiply both sides by 15 and 45.

$$2 \cdot 45 = 15x$$ Then simplify.

$$\frac{90}{15} = \frac{15x}{15}$$ Next, use inverse operations to solve for x. Divide both sides of the equation by 15.

$$x = 6$$ So, $x = 6$, which means $\frac{2}{15} = \frac{6}{45}$.

Solve each proportion for the variable.

$$\frac{6}{10} = \frac{q}{40}$$

$$\frac{3}{36} = \frac{1}{g}$$

$$\frac{8}{9} = \frac{p}{45}$$

$q =$ _____

$g =$ _____

$p =$ _____

$$\frac{5}{k} = \frac{30}{48}$$

$$\frac{m}{32} = \frac{20}{16}$$

$$\frac{21}{s} = \frac{6}{16}$$

$k =$ _____

$m =$ _____

$s =$ _____

IXL.com
skill ID
TDA

Keep going! Solve each proportion for the variable.

$\dfrac{27}{54} = \dfrac{3}{f}$

f = _____

$\dfrac{d}{44} = \dfrac{12}{16}$

d = _____

$\dfrac{2}{5} = \dfrac{n}{28}$

n = _____

$\dfrac{6}{b} = \dfrac{8}{38}$

b = _____

$\dfrac{16}{5} = \dfrac{a}{7}$

a = _____

$\dfrac{2}{y} = \dfrac{7}{10.5}$

y = _____

$\dfrac{1.5}{8} = \dfrac{0.6}{x}$

x = _____

$\dfrac{3.6}{9} = \dfrac{c}{95}$

c = _____

$\dfrac{v}{3.5} = \dfrac{7.6}{4}$

v = _____

> ## Learn!
>
> Two variables have a **proportional relationship** if all the ratios between them are equivalent.
>
> For example, this table represents a proportional relationship between x and y since all of the ratios are 3.
>
> If any of the ratios were different, the table would not represent a proportional relationship.

x	y	Ratio of y to x
3	9	$\frac{9}{3} = 3$
5	15	$\frac{15}{5} = 3$
10	30	$\frac{30}{10} = 3$

Determine whether each table represents a proportional relationship.

x	y	
2	8	$\frac{8}{2} = 4$
3	12	$\frac{12}{3} = 4$
5	15	$\frac{15}{5} = 3$

Yes   (No)

x	y
16	8
12	6
10	5

Yes   No

x	y
4	12
5	15
8	20

Yes   No

x	y
6	2
24	8
42	14

Yes   No

x	y
30	15
18	6
14	7

Yes   No

x	y
2	3
8	12
10	15

Yes   No

Keep going! Determine whether each table represents a proportional relationship.

x	y
8	6
12	9
20	15
36	27

Yes   No

x	y
1	4
2	9
3	14
4	19

Yes   No

x	y
2	4
3	9
5	25
12	144

Yes   No

x	y
13	39
26	78
29	87
$33\frac{1}{3}$	100

Yes   No

x	y
$1\frac{1}{2}$	$3\frac{3}{4}$
3	$7\frac{1}{2}$
18	45
36	90

Yes   No

x	y
$5\frac{1}{2}$	11
$6\frac{1}{2}$	12
$7\frac{1}{2}$	13
$8\frac{1}{2}$	14

Yes   No

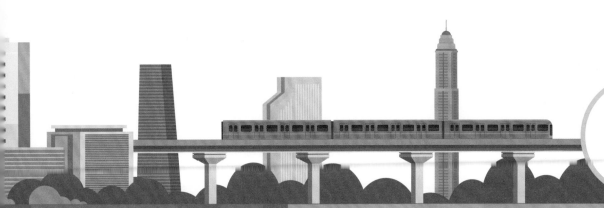

IXL.com
skill ID
6V7

In a proportional relationship, the ratio of *y* to *x* is called the **constant of proportionality**. It can be represented with the variable *k*.

Determine the constant of proportionality for each proportional relationship.

x	y	
2	10	$\frac{10}{2} = 5$
3	15	$\frac{15}{3} = 5$
5	25	$\frac{25}{5} = 5$
7	35	$\frac{35}{7} = 5$

k = ___5___

x	y
2	6
7	21
9	27
14	42

k = _____

x	y
2	12
5	30
6	36
7	42

k = _____

x	y
6	2
9	3
15	5
21	7

k = _____

x	y
16	24
24	36
32	48
40	60

k = _____

Keep going! Determine the constant of proportionality for each proportional relationship.

x	y
14	8
28	16
35	20
49	28

$k =$ _____

x	y
1	1.2
3	3.6
8	9.6
12	14.4

$k =$ _____

x	y
3	$2\frac{1}{2}$
6	5
5	$4\frac{1}{6}$
12	10

$k =$ _____

x	y
2.2	9.9
3.3	14.85
4.8	21.6
5.1	22.95

$k =$ _____

x	y
$\frac{1}{4}$	$\frac{3}{20}$
$1\frac{1}{2}$	$\frac{9}{10}$
6	$3\frac{3}{5}$
$8\frac{3}{4}$	$5\frac{1}{4}$

$k =$ _____

x	y
$3\frac{1}{4}$	26
$5\frac{1}{2}$	44
$6\frac{1}{8}$	49
$8\frac{1}{2}$	68

$k =$ _____

Learn!

A proportional relationship can be represented using an equation in the form **y = kx**, where k is the constant of proportionality.

You can write an equation for a proportional relationship shown in a table. First, find the constant of proportionality. Then, write the equation using the constant of proportionality.

In this table, the constant of proportionality is 2. So, the equation is $y = 2x$.

x	y
2	4
4	8
7	14

$\frac{y}{x} = k$

$\frac{4}{2} = 2$

$\frac{8}{4} = 2$

$\frac{14}{7} = 2$

Write an equation to represent each proportional relationship.

x	y
1	4
2	8
3	12

Equation: _____

x	y
5	45
6	54
9	81

Equation: _____

x	y
6	4
12	8
30	20

Equation: _____

x	y
4.2	12.6
5.1	15.3
7.8	23.4

Equation: _____

x	y
$\frac{1}{6}$	$\frac{1}{8}$
$\frac{1}{3}$	$\frac{1}{4}$
$\frac{1}{2}$	$\frac{3}{8}$

Equation: _____

IXL.com
skill ID
6GU

Write an equation for each proportional relationship.

Mark is mixing paint to create a new color. He uses 4 cups of blue paint and 3 cups of yellow paint. There is a proportional relationship between the amount of blue paint, x, and the amount of yellow paint, y.

Equation: _____

Sunny Days Art Camp has 4 counselors for 32 campers. There is a proportional relationship between the number of counselors, x, and the number of campers, y.

Equation: _____

Enrique paid $25.75 for 5 magazines. There is a proportional relationship between the number of magazines, x, and the cost, y.

Equation: _____

Mr. Dowd made 36 frozen ice pops using 6 ice pop molds. There is a proportional relationship between the number of molds, x, and the number of ice pops, y.

Equation: _____

Lin uses $\frac{1}{2}$ of a teaspoon of oregano for every $\frac{3}{4}$ of a teaspoon of basil in his favorite pasta sauce recipe. There is a proportional relationship between the amount of basil, x, and the amount of oregano, y.

Equation: _____

Write an equation for each proportional relationship. Then answer the question.

A lemonade recipe calls for 5 lemons and 2 cups of water. There is a proportional relationship between the number of lemons, x, and the number of cups of water, y.

Equation: _____

Josh is making a batch of lemonade that uses 8 cups of water. How many lemons will he need?

_____

At the spring carnival, it costs 18 tickets to play 6 games. There is a proportional relationship between the number of games, x, and the number of tickets, y.

Equation: _____

Jackie played 10 games at the carnival. How many tickets did she use?

_____

Garner Grounds is offering a deal on two-player board games. Jorge bought 3 of these board games for $31.50. There is a proportional relationship between the number of two-player board games, x, and the cost, y.

Equation: _____

How much would Jorge have paid if he bought 5 of the two-player board games?

_____

Priya used $22\frac{1}{2}$ square feet of fabric to make 5 purses to sell at the Creative Designs Craft Fair. There is a proportional relationship between the number of purses, x, and the number of square feet of fabric, y.

Equation: _____

How many purses can Priya make using 36 square feet of fabric?

_____

The graph of a proportional relationship is a straight line that passes through the origin.

Determine whether each graph represents a proportional relationship.

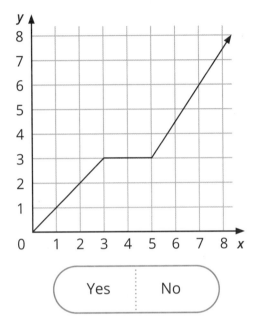

Yes   No

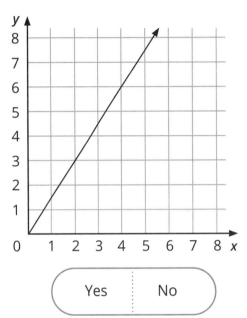

Yes   No

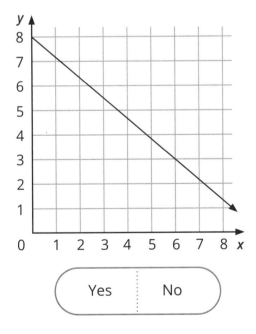

Yes   No

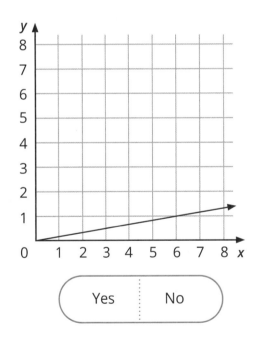

Yes   No

Graph the points from the table on the coordinate plane and connect the points with a line. Then determine whether the graph represents a proportional relationship.

x	y
2	5
3	6
4	7
5	8

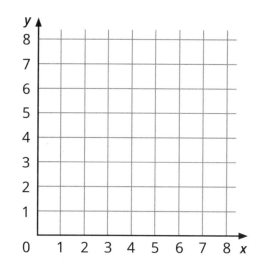

Yes | No

x	y
2	2
3	3
7	7
8	8

Yes | No

x	y
0	0
0.5	2
2	5
2.5	7

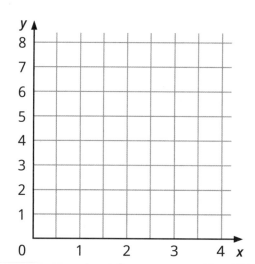

Yes | No

Keep going! Graph the points and determine whether the graph represents a proportional relationship.

x	y
2	4
2.5	5
3.5	7
4	8

Yes | No

x	y
3	12
6	10
9	8
15	4

Yes | No

x	y
4	5
6	10
12	15
16	20

Yes | No

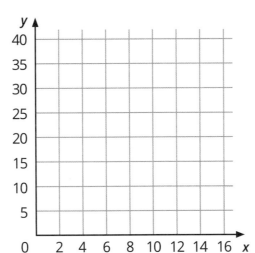

Learn!

Remember, in a proportional relationship, the ratio of *y* to *x* is the constant of proportionality, *k*. This is also the unit rate. To find *k* from a graph of a proportional relationship, choose a point on the graph and calculate the ratio of the *y*-coordinate to the *x*-coordinate. Look at the example below.

First, identify the coordinates of any point on the line other than the origin.

Then, calculate the ratio of the *y*-coordinate to the *x*-coordinate.

$$\frac{y\text{-coordinate}}{x\text{-coordinate}} = \frac{6}{4} = \frac{3}{2}$$

So, the constant of proportionality is $\frac{3}{2}$.

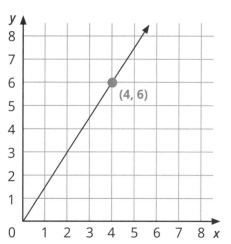

Determine the constant of proportionality for each graph.

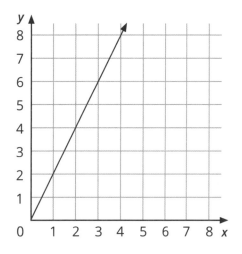

$k =$ _____

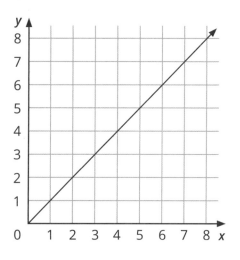

$k =$ _____

Keep going! Determine the constant of proportionality for each graph.

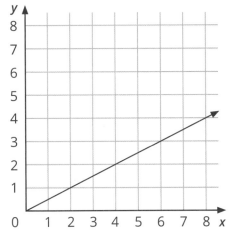

k = _____

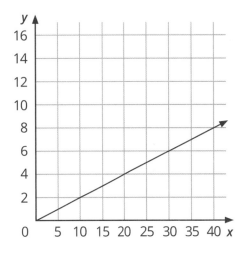

k = _____

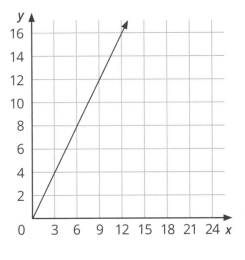

k = _____

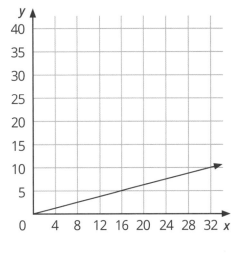

k = _____

Remember, a proportional relationship can be represented using the equation $y = kx$, where k is the constant of proportionality. You can write an equation for a proportional relationship shown in a graph.

Try it! Write an equation to represent each proportional relationship.

Luna is playing games at Frankfort Fun Park. There is a proportional relationship between the number of games, x, and the number of tokens, y, that she needs.

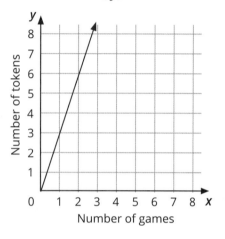

Equation: ___$y = 3x$___

Tony reserved some tables at Star Cafe for his birthday dinner. There is a proportional relationship between the number of tables, x, and the number of guests, y.

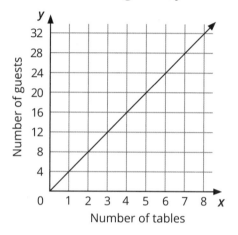

Equation: _____

Emmet is walking around the track at his school. There is a proportional relationship between the amount of time, x, and the number of miles, y.

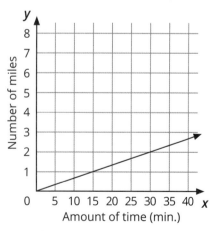

Equation: _____

Nature Trail's best selling product is trail mix. There is a proportional relationship between the number of cups of almonds, x, and the number of cups of peanuts, y, in the trail mix.

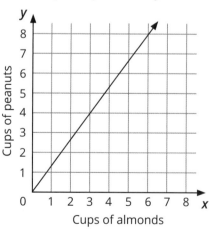

Equation: _____

Keep going! Write an equation to represent each proportional relationship.

Jayla made popcorn for her friends to eat while watching *Panda Quest*. There is a proportional relationship between the number of bags of popcorn, *x*, and the number of bowls they fill, *y*.

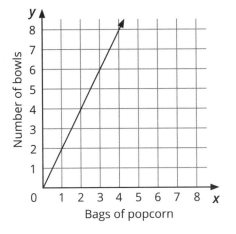

Equation: _____

Maren enjoys visiting Prairie Farm to pick strawberries. There is a proportional relationship between the number of pounds of strawberries, *x*, and the cost, *y*.

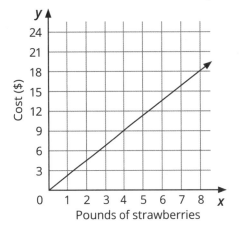

Equation: _____

Ms. Kyle made fruit punch for a graduation party. There is a proportional relationship between the number of cups of pineapple juice, *x*, and the number of cups of orange juice, *y*.

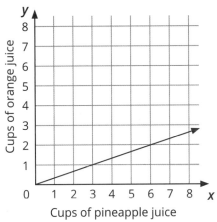

Equation: _____

IXL.com
skill ID
JKH

Use the graphs to answer the questions.

The graph shows the proportional relationship between the cups of carrots, *x*, and the cups of peas, *y*, in a vegetable medley.

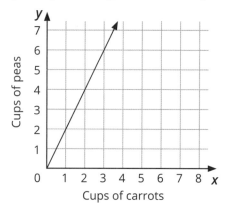

What does the point (3, 6) represent?

A vegetable medley with _____ cups of carrots also has _____ cups of peas.

What does the point (1, 2) represent?

A vegetable medley with _____ cup of carrots also has _____ cups of peas.

The graph shows the proportional relationship between the number of shelves, *x*, and the number of books on the shelves, *y*.

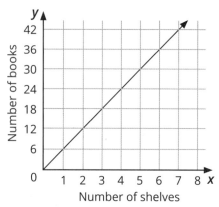

What does the point (5, 30) represent?

_____ shelves can hold _____ books.

What does the point (0, 0) represent?

_____ shelves can hold _____ books.

The graph shows the proportional relationship between the gallons of water in a fish tank, *x*, and the number of fish the tank can hold, *y*.

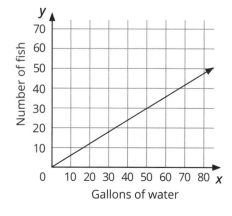

What does the point (50, 30) represent?

A fish tank with _____ gallons of water can hold _____ fish.

What does the point (25, 15) represent?

A fish tank with _____ gallons of water can hold _____ fish.

Keep going! Use the graphs to answer the questions.

The graph shows the proportional relationship between the number of videos recorded, *x*, and the total recording time in minutes, *y*.

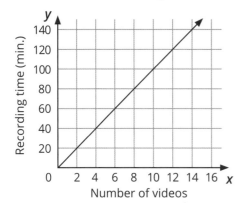

How many videos will be recorded in 80 minutes?

_____

How long does it take to record 1 video?

_____

The graph shows the proportional relationship between the number of fire trucks, *x*, and the number of race cars, *y*, in Mike's little brother's toy collection.

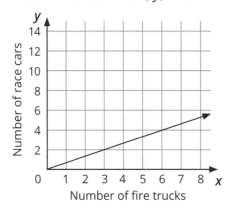

If Mike's brother has 2 race cars, how many fire trucks does he have?

_____

If Mike's brother has 9 fire trucks, how many race cars does he have?

_____

The graph shows the proportional relationship between the number of weeks Tanvi has been saving money, *x*, and her savings in dollars, *y*.

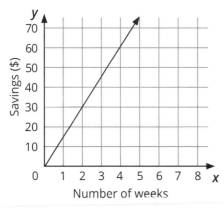

How many weeks did it take Tanvi to save $45?

_____

How much money did Tanvi save in 0 weeks?

_____

IXL.com
skill ID
RMH

The students at Rockstream Middle School are looking forward to the annual year-end track meet. The school's staff and members of the student council are helping prepare for the meet.

Ms. Hunter volunteered to order the ribbons for each event's top finishers. She will order 3 ribbons for every event in the meet. The relationship between the number of events, x, and the number of ribbons ordered, y, is proportional.

Write an equation with x and y to describe the relationship.

Equation: _____

Complete the table. Then graph the relationship on the coordinate plane.

Number of events	Number of ribbons ordered
1	
2	
3	
5	
7	

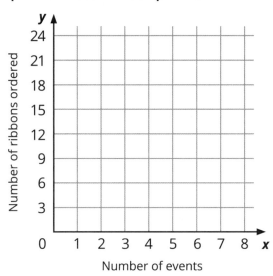

Answer each question.

Write the ordered pair of the point on the line with an x-coordinate of 4. (_____ , _____)

This point means that _____ ribbons would be ordered for _____ events.

Write the ordered pair of the point on the line with a y-coordinate of 18. (_____ , _____)

This point means that _____ ribbons

would be ordered for _____ events.

The student council members volunteered to prepare snacks for the track meet. They need to prepare 20 orange slices for every 5 students participating in the meet. The relationship between the number of students, x, and the number of orange slices needed, y, is proportional.

Write an equation with x and y to describe the relationship.

Equation: _____

Complete the table. Then graph the relationship on the coordinate plane.

Number of students	Number of orange slices
5	
10	
20	
25	
35	

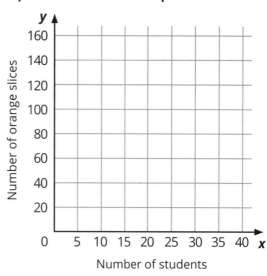

Answer each question.

How many orange slices are needed per student? _____

Write this as an ordered pair. (_____ , _____)

How many orange slices are needed for 24 students? _____

Write this as an ordered pair. (_____ , _____)

IXL.com skill ID

5DR

Complete the table by filling in the missing numbers.

Fraction	Decimal	Percent
$\frac{43}{100}$	0.43	43%
$\frac{9}{100}$		
	0.8	
$\frac{7}{20}$		
		25%
	0.01	
	0.64	
$\frac{13}{1,000}$		
		110%
	1.75	
$\frac{1}{8}$		

Learn!

You can solve percent problems using the **percent equation**, where the percent is written as a fraction or a decimal.

$$\text{part} = \text{percent} \times \text{whole}$$

Try it! What is 24% of 50? First, write the percent equation. The part is unknown, the percent is 24%, and the whole is 50. Then simplify.

$$\text{part} = 0.24 \times 50 = \mathbf{12}$$

So, 24% of 50 is 12.

Use the percent equation to solve each problem.

15% of 40 = _____

30% of 60 = _____

25% of 48 = _____

50% of 26 = _____

12% of 100 = _____

70% of 30 = _____

8% of 55 = _____

5.5% of 200 = _____

120% of 75 = _____

110% of 30 = _____

0.1% of 700 = _____

IXL.com
skill ID
93K

Learn!

You can also solve percent problems using the **percent proportion** to solve for an unknown part, whole, or percent.

$$\frac{\text{part}}{\text{whole}} = \frac{\text{percent}}{100}$$

Try this example: **60%** of **what number** is **3**?

First, set up the percent proportion. Write the part, 3, over the whole, which is unknown. Set that equal to the percent, 60, over 100.

$$\frac{3}{w} = \frac{60}{100}$$

Then, solve the same way you would solve a proportion.

$$3 \cdot 100 = 60w$$
$$\frac{300}{60} = \frac{60w}{60}$$

So, 60% of 5 is 3.

$$5 = w$$

Use the percent proportion to answer each question.

___20___% of 30 = 6

$$\frac{6}{30} = \frac{p}{100} \qquad 6 \cdot 100 = 30p$$
$$\frac{600}{30} = \frac{30p}{30}$$
$$20 = p$$

_____% of 40 = 18

75% of 32 = _____

_____% of 36 = 1.8

60% of 42 = _____

0.5% of _____ = 2

150% of _____ = 6

Use the menu to answer the questions. Round your answers to the nearest cent.

GreenPark Cafe just opened in Rafi's neighborhood. There is a 4.5% sales tax applied to all orders at the cafe.

WRAPS			SIDES		
Grilled Chicken	$8		Green Beans	$3
Veggie	$7		Fries	$4
Avocado	$12		Pasta Salad	$5
Hummus	$9		House Salad	$6

DESSERTS			DRINKS		
Pudding	$5		Berry Smoothie	$4
Carrot Cake	$6		Fresh Juice	$3
Brownie	$4		Bottled Water	$2
Apple Crisp	$7		Herbal Tea	$2

Rafi ordered a veggie wrap, fries, and a fresh juice. How much did he pay in tax?

_____

Miranda chose an avocado wrap, a house salad, a bottled water, and a brownie. She decided to leave a 15% tip on the cost of her food before tax. How much was the tip?

_____

Val had a grilled chicken wrap and a berry smoothie. If Val added a 12% tip to the cost of her food before tax, how much did she pay for the tax and tip together?

_____

Max picked up an order for himself and his brother. The order contained 2 hummus wraps, 2 pasta salads, a slice of carrot cake, a berry smoothie, and a bottled water. Max and his brother decided to split the total cost of the food, including tax. How much did each of them pay?

_____

IXL.com
skill ID
Y5R

Learn!

The **percent of change** tells you the percent that an original amount increased or decreased. To find the percent of change, find the amount of change by subtracting the smaller amount from the larger amount. Then, divide that by the original amount.

$$\text{percent of change} = \frac{\text{amount of change}}{\text{original amount}}$$

When the new amount is greater than the original amount, it is a **percent increase**. When the new amount is less than the original amount, it is a **percent decrease**.

Try it! What is the percent of change from 70 to 77? Divide the amount of change by the original amount. Then, simplify and write your answer as a percent.

$$\text{percent of change} = \frac{77 - 70}{70} = \frac{7}{70} = \frac{1}{10} \text{ or } 10\%$$

The new amount is greater than the original, so the percent of change is a 10% increase.

Fill in the table.

Original amount	Percent of change	New amount
100	25% decrease	75
50		60
30		12
48		42
12		30

IXL.com
skill ID
BL7

Learn!

You can also calculate the original amount before a percent increase or decrease. Try it! Find the original price of a sweater that is on sale for $30, which is 25% less than its original price.

First, decide if there was a percent increase or decrease. "25% less" means there was a percent decrease. So, subtract 25% of the original amount from 100% of the original amount.

100% − 25% = 75%

Then, write an equation to show that the sale price of the sweater, $30, is 75% of the original price, x. Make sure to write the percent as a decimal.

$30 = 0.75x$

Use inverse operations to solve for x.

$$\frac{30}{0.75} = \frac{0.75x}{0.75}$$

So, $40 = x$, which means the original price of the sweater was $40.

$40 = x$

Answer each question.

Brandi purchased an acrylic paint set for $56. It was on sale for 30% off. What was the original price of the paint set?

_____

Smith Middle School's basketball team scored 44 points in tonight's game, which was 10% more than the previous game. How many points did the team score in the previous game?

_____

Lea was only able to spend 16 hours working on puzzles this month, which is 48.8% less time than last month. How many hours did Lea spend working on puzzles last month?

_____

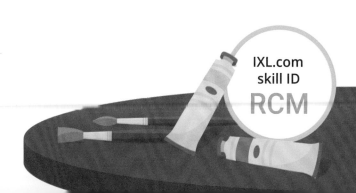

IXL.com
skill ID
RCM

Determine the better discount.

Layla wants to buy a guitar originally priced at $129. She has two coupons from Music Place. Which coupon should Layla use to save the most money?

$35 off any guitar | (30% off any instrument)

Mr. Conway needs a new printer for his home office. He has two coupons to choose from. Which should he use to get the best deal on a $259 printer?

$40 off any printer | 15% off any purchase

Andy needs a larger tent for his next camping trip. He found a tent that costs $319, and it is on sale at two different stores. Which discount will give Andy the best price?

$25 off any tent | 10% off any tent

Zach is joining a gym that is offering a discount this month on its $330 yearly membership. He also received a coupon in the mail with a different discount for the gym membership. Which will give him a lower price to join the gym?

$30 off new memberships | 9% discount for new memberships

Frank receives coupons by email and text for his favorite Mexican restaurant. If he spends $35 on a meal, which coupon should Frank use?

$5 off any meal | 5% off any meal

A **discount** is a decrease from the original price, while a **markup** is an increase from the original price. Use what you know about solving percent problems to answer each question.

Serena is shopping at a store where all of the winter clothes are on sale. An $89 jacket has been discounted by 30%. How much will Serena pay for the jacket?

_____

Going Places Bike Shop pays $23 for a tricycle and sells it for $41.40. What is the percent markup on the tricycle?

_____

Cara waited in a long line for discounted tickets to see her favorite musical. She purchased $90 tickets for $32.40 each. What percent discount did Cara receive?

_____

A local grocery store purchases snacks from a distributor and marks them up by 22% before selling them. How much does the store charge for a bag of chips it gets for $1.50?

_____

Martina paid $53.55 for a set of books from her favorite mystery series during a 15% off sale. How much did the set cost without the discount?

_____

Learn!

When estimating, you will not always guess the exact amount. The **percent error** tells you by what percent your estimation is off. To find the percent error, find the amount of error, or the amount that the estimation differs from the actual amount. Then, divide that by the actual amount. The percent error will always be positive.

$$\text{percent error} = \frac{\text{amount of error}}{\text{actual amount}}$$

Answer each question. Round your answer to the nearest percent if needed.

Manuel expected to join 1 club in middle school, but he ended up joining 4 clubs. What was the percent error in Manuel's estimate?

_____75%_____

$$\frac{4-1}{4} = \frac{3}{4} = 0.75 \text{ or } 75\%$$

Aaron estimated he could hike for 6 miles, but he was able to hike for 10 miles. What was the percent error in Aaron's estimate?

_____

Clare thought she would score 155 points in the bowling tournament. She came close, scoring 149 points. What was the percent error in Clare's estimate?

_____

Sebastian's bus ride took 48 minutes on a high-traffic day. He had estimated it would only take 40 minutes. What was the percent error in Sebastian's estimate?

_____

Maura expected that her restaurant bill would be $24, but it was actually $32. What was the percent error in Maura's estimate?

_____

IXL.com
skill ID
6UY

Time for review! Solve each percent problem to complete the crossword puzzle. Each digit, decimal point, and dollar sign goes in its own box.

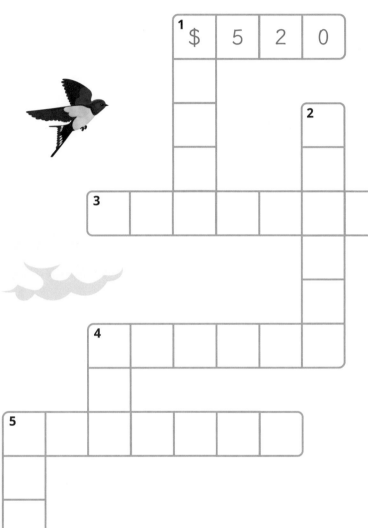

Across

1. A 13% commission on a $4,000 sale $= \$520$

3. A $145 basketball hoop after a 25% discount

4. A $39 pair of jeans with 5% sales tax

5. A 50% discount on a ring priced at $1,018.40

Down

1. The 6% tax on a $45 meal

2. A 21% commission on an $85 sale

4. The 20% tip on a $150 meal

5. The 28% markup on a $179 table

IXL.com
skill ID
ZHX

Learn!

Simple interest is money paid or earned on the principal, or starting amount, of an account. To find simple interest, use the formula below.

$$i = prt$$

i = interest earned
p = principal
r = interest rate written as a decimal
t = time in years

Try it! Maria deposits $400 into a savings account that earns 3% simple interest each year. How much interest will she earn over 5 years, assuming she does not add or take out any money?

$$i = prt$$
$$i = 400 \cdot 0.03 \cdot 5$$
$$i = 60$$

So, Maria will earn $60 in interest.

Answer each question.

Mr. Spier took out a $15,000 loan to replace the windows in his house. He agreed to pay back the loan plus 7% simple interest at the end of 3 years. How much interest did Mr. Spier pay?

_____

Joe put $5,000 into an account that paid 9% simple interest. What was the balance in the account after 2 years, assuming he did not add or take out any money?

_____

Raymond set aside $750 in a savings account that paid 4.5% simple interest. If he did not deposit or withdraw any money, what was the balance in the account after 6 years?

_____

Rooms for You offers buyers a loan with 1.8% simple interest for 5 years. Shay used this loan to purchase $3,800 of furniture. How much interest did she pay after 5 years?

_____

Exploration Zone

With simple interest, money is paid or earned only on the starting amount, or principal. With **compound interest**, money is paid or earned on the starting amount and on any interest earned. So compound interest can be thought of as "interest on interest." The longer the money is in an account, the more the money will grow.

TRY IT YOURSELF!

Complete the table below for a $1,000 deposit in an account earning 10% compound interest every year.

	Starting amount	Interest	Balance
Year 1	$1,000	$1,000 × 0.1 = $100	$1,000 + $100 = $1,100
Year 2	$1,100		
Year 3			
Year 4			
Year 5			

Answer the questions.

How much compound interest was earned in this account over 5 years? _____

If this account had 10% simple interest, how much interest would be earned over 5 years? _____

What is one situation where you might **want** compound interest? What is one situation where you might **not want** compound interest?

_____

_____

_____

IXL.com skill ID EHZ

Answer the questions about each expression.

$4a - 7d + 20$

How many terms are in the expression? _____3_____

What are the variables? __a__ and __d__

What is the coefficient of the second term? _____−7_____

$-3c - 6t - 10$

What is the constant term in this expression? _____

What is the coefficient of the first term? _____

What are the variables? _____ and _____

$-5.8 + 0.6q + 23.1b$

What is the constant term in the expression? _____

How many terms are in the expression? _____

What is the coefficient of the last term? _____

$\frac{1}{5}x + y + 2k - 6\frac{4}{7}$

How many terms in the expression contain variables? _____

What is the coefficient of the second term? _____

What is the constant term in the expression? _____

IXL.com
skill ID

E7H

$4\frac{1}{3} - 2j^2 - \frac{1}{4}w^2 + 11$

What are the variables? _____ and _____

What is the coefficient of the third term? _____

How many terms are in the expression? _____

Evaluate each expression using the given value.

$9c - 4$ for $c = 4$

$9(4) - 4 = 36 - 4 = 32$

$2p + 8$ for $p = -6$

$-6t - 10$ for $t = -1.5$

$\frac{3}{4}m - \frac{1}{2}$ for $m = 5$

$12 - 3x$ for $x = -\frac{3}{8}$

$\frac{3q}{5} + 6$ for $q = -10$

Keep going! Evaluate each expression using the given values.

$-3 - 0.2b - 1.3a$ for $b = -15$ and $a = 10$

$20 - 10r - 12s$ for $r = \frac{2}{5}$ and $s = -\frac{1}{2}$

$-7u + 6 + 8w$ for $u = 0.5$ and $w = -0.4$

Learn!

You can use the **distributive property** to expand expressions that are written as products. Look at the example.

$$3(n + 4) = 3(n) + 3(4)$$ Multiply each term in the parentheses by 3.
$$= 3n + 12$$ Then simplify.

Use the distributive property to expand each expression.

$-8(x + 3) = \underline{\quad -8x - 24 \quad}$

$4(t - 5) = \underline{\hspace{3cm}}$

$6(m + 1) = \underline{\hspace{3cm}}$

$-3(2v - 4) = \underline{\hspace{3cm}}$

$-4(8 + 3q) = \underline{\hspace{3cm}}$

$12(2f + 3) = \underline{\hspace{3cm}}$

$-2(1 + n) = \underline{\hspace{3cm}}$

$(8b - 6)(7) = \underline{\hspace{3cm}}$

$(-c + 1)(-4) = \underline{\hspace{3cm}}$

$6(7g - 6) = \underline{\hspace{3cm}}$

$-9(-5 + 9a) = \underline{\hspace{3cm}}$

IXL.com
skill ID
NUY

Keep going! Use the distributive property to expand each expression.

$16(5 - 3p) =$ _____

$0.5(-6c - 26) =$ _____

$-8\left(\dfrac{3}{8}a + \dfrac{1}{4}\right) =$ _____

$\dfrac{4}{9}(27h - 9) =$ _____

$-\dfrac{4}{5}(10 - 15p) =$ _____

$(-7t + 4)(0.6) =$ _____

$1.1(n + 3j - 10) =$ _____

$-\dfrac{3}{4}(28b - 20z + 4) =$ _____

$-\dfrac{1}{6}(12s - 30 - 6q) =$ _____

$-5(4.2 + 3.4j + m) =$ _____

76 Factoring expressions

Learn!

If the terms in an expression share a common factor, you can **factor** that expression. This means you can rewrite it as a product. Try it with $6x + 21$.

First, find the greatest common factor (GCF) of all the terms. The GCF of $6x$ and 21 is 3.	$\mathbf{6x + 21}$
Next, rewrite each term with the GCF, 3, as a factor.	$\mathbf{3(2x) + 3(7)}$
Then, factor out the GCF to rewrite the expression as a product.	$\mathbf{3(2x + 7)}$

Factor each expression.

$6x + 18 =$ ________________

$14y + 7 =$ ________________

$5q - 80 =$ ________________

$26t - 13 =$ ________________

$16 - 4n =$ ________________

$70 - 60k =$ ________________

$48 - 72w =$ ________________

$81g + 45 =$ ________________

$24p - 54 =$ ________________

Keep going! Factor each expression. Make sure to find the GCF of all three terms in the expression.

$4c - 6s + 8 =$ _____

$6q + 12w + 3m =$ _____

$48r - 16 - 40d =$ _____

$44 - 99b - 33t =$ _____

$81k - 9g + 27h =$ _____

$42 - 49a - 84x =$ _____

$8 + 16w - 12v =$ _____

$30u - 18t - 42 =$ _____

$26n + 34y - 2p =$ _____

TAKE ANOTHER LOOK!

Check your answers by using the distributive property. You should get the original expression!

IXL.com
skill ID
J9G

Simplify each expression by combining like terms.

$3x + 8x - 12 = $ ___11x − 12___

$p + 6p - 2p = $ _____

$20g - 6 - 4g = $ _____

$-5c + 9c + 2k = $ _____

$17s - 18s + s + 4 = $ _____

$12 + 8t + 18 + 22t = $ _____

$3 - m + 2m + 6 + 2m = $ _____

$4v + 4d - v - 5d + 1 = $ _____

$7t - 8y - t + 3y + 2 = $ _____

$-2k + 3j - 6k + 4k = $ _____

$\frac{3}{4}r + \frac{1}{4}r - 2r + 5 = $ _____

$1.5g - 2h + 4.9g - h = $ _____

IXL.com
skill ID
JJG

For more practice, visit IXL.com or the IXL mobile app and enter this code in the search bar.

Draw a line between each pair of equivalent expressions.

$3t + \dfrac{1}{2}(4t - 8) + 6$ $3t - 6$

$19t + 2\dfrac{1}{4} - 14t + 1\dfrac{3}{4}$ $5t + 2$

$-3t - 6t - 8 + 12t + 2$ $4t + 2$

$6(4 - 3t) + 20t - 20$ $5t + 4$

$0.6 - 3t + 1.4 + 7t$ $7t + 15$

$2t + 5(t + 3)$ $4 + 2t$

Learn!

You can add linear expressions using the properties of operations. Look at the example.

First, identify like terms.	$(4p - 6) + (-p + 2)$
Then, use the commutative and associative properties to reorder and group like terms.	$(4p + (-p)) + (-6 + 2)$
Next, combine like terms.	$3p + (-4)$
Simplify, if needed. You may need to rewrite the addition as subtraction.	$3p - 4$

Add the linear expressions.

$(4x - 3) + (2x + 5) = $ _____ $(6y + 5) + (-2) = $ _____

$(7 - h) + (3h - 2) = $ _____ $(5.3 + 9p) + (7.2p + 5) = $ _____

$(12n - 3j) + (j - 2n) = $ _____ $\left(\frac{1}{3}a + 4z\right) + \left(4z + \frac{1}{6}a\right) = $ _____

$(8f - 7) + (3f + 2v + 10.4) = $ _____

Learn!

You can also subtract linear expressions using the properties of operations. Look at the example.

First, rewrite subtraction as addition. Remember, subtraction is the same as adding the opposite.

$$(7q - 8) - (-2q - 4)$$

$$(7q - 8) + (-1)(-2q - 4)$$

You can use the distributive property to distribute –1 to each term in the second expression.

$$(7q - 8) + (-1)(-2q) + (-1)(-4)$$

Then, simplify and identify like terms.

$$(7q - 8) + (2q + 4)$$

Next, use the commutative and associative properties to reorder and group like terms.

$$(7q + 2q) + (-8 + 4)$$

Finally, combine like terms. Simplify, if needed.

$$9q + (-4)$$

$$9q - 4$$

Subtract the linear expressions.

$(4c + 8) - (c) =$ _____

$(8 - 2a) - (6a) =$ _____

$(6s + 4.3) - (3s + 5.9) =$ _____

$\left(\dfrac{1}{2}t + 8\right) - \left(-1 + \dfrac{3}{8}t\right) =$ _____

$(3 - 2v) - (4v + 8 - 1.2w) =$ _____

IXL.com
skill ID
6BT

Circle all of the expressions that represent the given situation.

Gabby's haircut cost b dollars, and she wants to tip her stylist. If Gabby leaves a 30% tip, circle all of the expressions that represent the total amount she paid.

$b(1 + 0.3)$	$b + 30$	$b + 0.3b$	$1.3b$

Last weekend, Lola spent m minutes practicing the violin and 40 minutes reading. This weekend, Lola spent twice as much time practicing the violin and 20 fewer minutes reading. Circle all of the expressions that represent the total amount of time Lola spent on those activities this weekend.

$2m + 20$	$2m + 40 - 20$	$2(m + 40) - 20$	$m + 40 + m - 20$

Jamal has been waiting for a gaming system to go on sale. The gaming system costs p dollars, and it is finally on sale for 15% off. Circle all of the expressions that represent the sale price.

$0.85p$	$0.15p$	$p(1 + 0.15)$	$p - 0.15p$

Makayla recently joined her school's softball team. During each practice, she runs laps for 10 minutes and works on drills for d minutes. If Makayla practiced 3 times last week, circle all of the expressions that represent the total amount of minutes she spent practicing last week.

$30d$	$3(d + 10)$	$3d + 30$	$3 + d + 10$

IXL.com
skill ID
KWH

DIG DEEPER! Write a different equivalent expression for each of the situations above.

It's time for the drama club to start preparing for the school play! For each problem below, write two different expressions that represent the situation. Then, evaluate one of your expressions for the given value.

Nicole is handling ticket sales. She expects a 5% increase in ticket sales this year compared to last year, when *t* tickets were sold. Write two different expressions that represent the predicted sales for this year.

	Find the predicted sales if *t* = 320.

Roy is in charge of costumes. He plans to buy the costumes at Costumes Galore, where he has a 20% off coupon. If the costumes cost *c* dollars before the discount, write two different expressions that represent the cost of Roy's purchase after the discount.

	Find the discounted cost if *c* = 465.80.

Rita is in charge of the stage crew. She needs *g* students to work on the lights, half as many students to work on sound, and 12 students to paint the sets. Write two different expressions that represent the total number of students needed for the stage crew.

	Find the total number of students if *g* = 4.

IXL.com
skill ID
XMD

Use inverse operations to solve each equation.

$t + 8 = 15$
$\underline{-8 \quad -8}$
$\quad t = 7$

$w - 6 = 4$

$7 + q = -3$

$-6 = x - 3$

$p - (-3) = 5$

$m + 15 = 9$

$-11 + s = -5$

$z - 8.5 = 3.4$

$16.7 = n + 5.2$

$d + \dfrac{3}{5} = \dfrac{9}{10}$

$b - \dfrac{1}{4} = \dfrac{2}{3}$

$-6.3 + v = -4.9$

$\dfrac{1}{4} = 2 + f$

$y + 3\dfrac{2}{3} = 1\dfrac{5}{12}$

$-7.34 + h = -0.9$

Keep going! Use inverse operations to solve each equation.

$\dfrac{6s}{6} = \dfrac{18}{6}$

$s = 3$

$\dfrac{m}{4} = 8$

$-7a = 14$

$\dfrac{f}{2} = -12$

$-3k = -33$

$-\dfrac{p}{5} = 3$

$-4g = -2.8$

$-8 = -\dfrac{n}{9}$

$46 = -2x$

$0.2c = 6.4$

$-3 = \dfrac{y}{7.2}$

$-\dfrac{2}{3}j = -50$

$\dfrac{4}{3}t = \dfrac{8}{9}$

$-8.25 = 2.5r$

$9v = \dfrac{3}{4}$

Solve each equation. Use the answers to draw a path from start to finish.

START

$-4 + x = 4$		$9x = -3$		$\dfrac{x}{9} = 6$		$x - 4 = -2$
	0		$\dfrac{1}{3}$		14	

8   -7   -3   3/2 $\dfrac{2}{3}$ 5   -9

$x - 7 = -11$		$x + (-6) = 5$		$\dfrac{x}{4} = \dfrac{3}{16}$		$-\dfrac{3}{8}x = 6$
	4		13		$\dfrac{3}{4}$	

5.9   -4   -11   12   -3   -18   -16

$\dfrac{x}{4} = 4.5$		$\dfrac{7}{2}x = 35$		$x - (-6) = 3$		$-6.7 + x = -10$
	5		$2\dfrac{1}{2}$		3.3	

3   1.5   10   -0.9   3   -3.3   -1.3

$0.75x = 2.5$		$x + 1.6 = 0.7$		$x - 2\dfrac{2}{3} = \dfrac{7}{12}$		FINISH
	-2.3		2.3		$3\dfrac{1}{4}$	

Write an equation for each problem. Then solve.

A panda was born at Leighsville Zoo. In August, the panda weighed 2.7 pounds. Today, he weighs 18 pounds. How many pounds, p, did the panda gain between August and today?

$$2.7 + p = 18$$
$$2.7 - 2.7 + p = 18 - 2.7$$
$$p = 15.3$$

$\underline{2.7 + p = 18}$

$\underline{15.3 \text{ pounds}}$

Amsterville Road is under construction. Workers have paved 4 miles of the road, which is 12 miles less than the total length of the road. How many miles long, m, is the road?

A winter storm is approaching Morristown, and the temperature is dropping at a rate of 3°F per hour. How many hours, h, will it take for the temperature to drop 18°F?

A scuba diver dove down 12 meters to reach a tropical reef 39 meters below the surface of the water. What was the scuba diver's position, n, relative to the surface before the dive?

Jennie bought a bag of jelly beans from Sweet Tooth Confectionery. There are 14 cherry jelly beans in the bag. If $\frac{2}{5}$ of the bag is cherry, how many total jelly beans, j, are in the bag?

IXL.com
skill ID
BXY

Learn!

You can also use inverse operations to solve equations with more than one step. Remember, whatever you do to one side of the equation, you must also do to the other side. Try it! Solve $5x + 6 = 51$.

$$5x + 6 = 51$$

$$5x + 6 - 6 = 51 - 6$$ Subtract 6 from both sides of the equation. Then simplify.

$$5x = 45$$

$$\frac{5x}{5} = \frac{45}{5}$$ Divide both sides of the equation by 5. Then simplify.

$$x = 9$$

Solve each equation.

$4y + 8 = 20$ $5f - 6 = 14$ $3w - 17 = 16$

$-2h + 10 = 6$ $19 = 8b + 51$ $9k - 54 = -9$

$3d - 43 = -22$ $97 = -32m - 95$ $17t + 50 = -86$

Keep going! Solve each equation.

$\frac{1}{3}c - 4 = 5$

$-2v + 6.5 = -7.1$

$-8 = 4 + \frac{1}{8}u$

$0.4x + 7 = 19$

$-13 - \frac{1}{4}q = 7$

$-1.5g - 38.7 = 21.3$

$\frac{1}{2}n - 9\frac{1}{8} = 1\frac{7}{8}$

$\frac{2}{5}s - \frac{1}{2} = -\frac{1}{3}$

TAKE ANOTHER LOOK! Go back to the first problem on this page. Check your work by substituting the value of the variable into the original equation and simplifying.

IXL.com
skill ID
CMX

Learn!

When solving an equation with parentheses, you can use the distributive property to expand the expression. Then use inverse operations to isolate the variable. Try it! Solve $2(b - 6) = 14$.

$$2(b - 6) = 14$$

$$2(b) + 2(-6) = 14$$ Use the distributive property. Distribute 2 to each term inside the parentheses. Then simplify.

$$2b - 12 = 14$$

$$2b - 12 + 12 = 14 + 12$$ Add 12 to both sides. Then simplify.

$$2b = 26$$

$$\frac{2b}{2} = \frac{26}{2}$$ Divide both sides of the equation by 2. Then simplify.

$$b = 13$$

Solve each equation by distributing first.

$$4(k + 1) = 24$$
$$4k + 4 = 24$$
$$4k + 4 - 4 = 24 - 4$$
$$\frac{4k}{4} = \frac{20}{4}$$
$$k = 5$$

$$-3(w + 10) = -21$$

$$63 = 7(p - 11)$$

Try it another way! Solve each equation by dividing first.

$$\frac{8(t - 3)}{8} = \frac{72}{8}$$
$$t - 3 = 9$$
$$t - 3 + 3 = 9 + 3$$
$$t = 12$$

$$3(f + 3) = -45$$

$$-4(u - 18) = 16$$

IXL.com
skill ID
NSH

You decide! Solve each equation. You can distribute or divide first.

$4(w + 1.1) = 20.8$

$\frac{1}{4}(4 + 8a) = 15$

$\frac{2}{7}(14y - 21) = 24$

$57 = 3(c + 21.1)$

$-2(n + 12.5) = 3$

$-\frac{5}{6}(6v + 18) = 40$

$-\frac{2}{3}(j - 81) = 42$

$5(0.4g - 3.2) = 34.6$

$12(s - 1.2) = 45.6$

Time for review! Solve each equation.

$7f - 30 = 19$

$2(2w + 4) = -12$

$-9 = -8g - 12$

$-2\left(t - \dfrac{1}{2}\right) = -17$

$0.4j + 1 = -2$

$6\left(y + 2\dfrac{2}{3}\right) = 20$

$43 = -3\left(n - 6\dfrac{1}{3}\right)$

$0.8(p - 9.1) = 0.88$

$2d - 11\dfrac{1}{4} = \dfrac{1}{2}$

IXL.com
skill ID
QEB

Draw a line between each equation and its solution.

$7(m - 6) = -91$ $m = -4$

$44 = 9m + 80$ $m = 6$

$-63 = 4m - 83$ $m = -7$

$4(2 - 2m) = 56$ $m = -6$

$-12m + 88 = 16$ $m = 5$

Crack the code by solving each equation! Then look for any places where that solution appears in the code at the bottom of the page, and write the corresponding letter on the line. Use the code to reveal the rest of the joke! Not every letter will be used in the code at the bottom.

O	$5x + 2 = 27$	**A**	$3(x - 8) = -12$
T	$0.25(x - 5) = 3$	**I**	$\frac{1}{4}x + 5 = 1$
V	$4 = 3x - 14$	**E**	$-32 = -2(x + 7)$
M	$-\frac{1}{6}x + 7 = -9$	**N**	$\frac{3}{4}x - 7 = 8$
D	$\frac{3}{5}(x - 15) = -15$	**S**	$2.4 - 0.3x = 4.5$

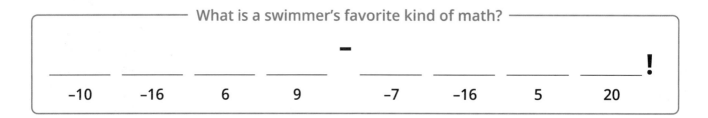

What is a swimmer's favorite kind of math?

____ ____ ____ ____ **–** ____ ____ ____ ____!

–10   –16   6   9   –7   –16   5   20

Learn!

When solving an equation with like terms, you can combine like terms first. Then use inverse operations to isolate the variable. Try it! Solve $4t - 6 - 2t + 10 = 14$.

$4t - 6 - 2t + 10 = 14$ Combine like terms, paying attention to the signs. $4t$ and $-2t$ are like terms, and -6 and 10 are like terms.

$2t + 4 = 14$

$2t + 4 - 4 = 14 - 4$ Next, use inverse operations to solve. Subtract 4 from both sides. Then simplify.

$2t = 10$

$\dfrac{2t}{2} = \dfrac{10}{2}$ Divide both sides of the equation by 2. Then simplify.

$t = 5$

Solve each equation.

$3y + 5y = 64$

$9g - 2g + 3g = 120$

$-6m - 14m - 8 = 72$

$2a + 8 - 4a - 2 = 36$

$12p + 3p - 26 + 6p - 5 = 11$

IXL.com
skill ID
VSW

Write an equation for each problem.

Ms. Stone is planning Oak Middle School's talent show. She wants each of the 10 students to have an equal amount of time on stage. The show will be 90 minutes long including a 20-minute intermission. How much time, t, will each student have on stage?

$$10t + 20 = 90$$

Alvin's family is going on a trip to Alaska, and all 5 family members need to buy winter hats. They used a coupon for $15 off their entire purchase, and the total came to $89 before tax. If each hat cost the same price, p, what was the price of each hat?

_____

Jada's class collected 60 nonperishable food items for a local food pantry. Jada and her friend each donated n items. If the rest of their class donated 46 items, how many items did Jada and her friend each donate?

_____

The Platt family ordered 4 large pizzas, each with a different topping, and spent $55.60. The price of a large pizza without any toppings is $10.95. If all toppings cost the same amount, c, what is the price of each topping?

_____

IXL.com
skill ID
8NH

Darrell sold cookies and brownies at a bake sale for $1.25 each and earned a total of $83.75. If he sold 24 cookies, how many brownies, b, did he sell?

_____

Write an equation for each problem. Then solve.

Barry bought 4 T-shirts that each cost the same amount, and he paid $3.60 in sales tax. If Barry paid a total of $63.56 after tax, what was the cost of each T-shirt, t, before tax?

_____$14.99_____

$$4t + 3.60 = 63.56$$
$$4t + 3.60 - 3.60 = 63.56 - 3.60$$
$$\frac{4t}{4} = \frac{59.96}{4}$$
$$t = 14.99$$

Bella's Boutique is having its annual sale where every item in the store is marked down. During the sale, bracelets sell for $10 less than full price. Amy purchases 4 charm bracelets. She pays a total of $60. What is the full price, b, of each bracelet?

_____

Kami is saving money to buy a new computer. She has $235 in her savings account. Each week, Kami deposits $20 into the account. If the computer costs $875, how many weeks, w, will it take for Kami to have enough money for the computer?

_____

A baker used 16 cups of flour to bake cookies and the rest of the bag to bake 96 muffins. If there were 40 cups of flour in the bag to start, how much flour, f, was used for each muffin?

_____

IXL.com
skill ID
D2Y

Graph each inequality on the number line.

$x > 4$

$x < -2$

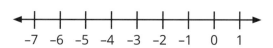

$x \leq 7$

$x \geq -5$

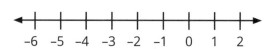

$x > 5\frac{1}{2}$

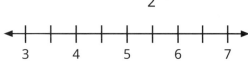

$x \geq 2.7$

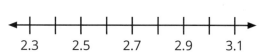

$x \leq -1.8$

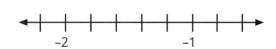

$x \geq -\frac{3}{5}$

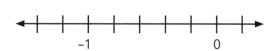

Write the inequality shown.

$$\underline{\quad x \ \geq \ -1 \quad}$$

_____

_____

_____

_____

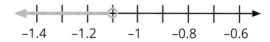

_____

_____

_____

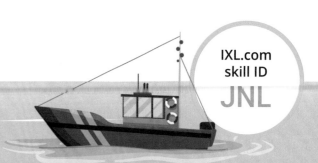

IXL.com
skill ID

JNL

A **solution** to an inequality is a value for the variable that makes the inequality true. Circle all of the solutions for each inequality.

$x > 3$		$y \leq 9$	
$x = 2$	$x = -4$	$y = -2$	$y = -11$
$x = 7$	$x = 3$	$y = 9$	$y = -9$

$-2 + z \geq 2$		$m - 1 < -4$	
$z = 4$	$z = -1$	$m = -8$	$m = -2$
$z = 2$	$z = 5$	$m = -5$	$m = -3$

$5 - t \geq 0$		$8q < 1$	
$t = 0$	$t = 6$	$q = -8$	$q = 8$
$t = 5$	$t = -6$	$q = 10$	$q = -2$

$3 + r \leq -1$		$\dfrac{p}{2} > -5$	
$r = -3$	$r = -5$	$p = 5$	$p = 10$
$r = -4$	$r = -1$	$p = -8$	$p = -10$

Learn!

You can solve an inequality with addition or subtraction by using inverse operations to isolate the variable. Look at the examples.

$$r + 2 > 7$$
$$r + 2 - 2 > 7 - 2$$
$$r > 5$$

$$6 \geq t - 2$$
$$6 + 2 \geq t - 2 + 2$$
$$8 \geq t \text{ or } t \leq 8$$

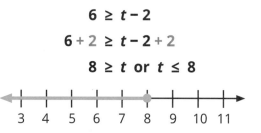

Be careful: If you rewrite the inequality with the variable on the opposite side, you must flip the inequality sign. This is why you can rewrite $8 \geq t$ as $t \leq 8$ in the second example above.

Solve each inequality. Then graph the solution set on the number line.

$$x - 3 > 2$$

$$m - 9 < -1$$

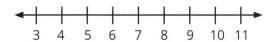

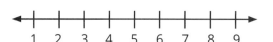

$$-4 + b > -9$$

$$6 \leq a - 1$$

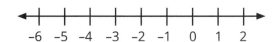

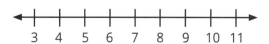

$$p + \frac{1}{2} \geq 5$$

$$-6.7 > k - 5.1$$

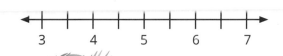

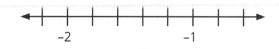

Learn!

You can also use inverse operations to solve an inequality with multiplication or division. Look at the examples.

$-2x > -12$

$\dfrac{-2x}{-2} < \dfrac{-12}{-2}$

$x < 6$

Be careful: If you multiply or divide by a negative number, you must flip the inequality sign!

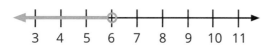

$\dfrac{y}{2} \geq 3$

$2 \cdot \dfrac{y}{2} \geq 2 \cdot 3$

$y \geq 6$

Solve each inequality. Then graph the solution set on the number line.

$5f < 25$

$\dfrac{g}{4} \geq 1$

$\dfrac{n}{2} > -1.5$

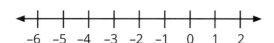

$-3d < 6$

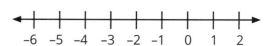

$-\dfrac{v}{5} \leq -\dfrac{3}{10}$

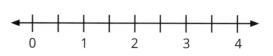

Keep going! Solve each inequality and graph the solution set on the number line.

$q + 4.3 > 2.3$

$b - \dfrac{5}{6} < 2\dfrac{1}{6}$

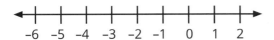

$-9f \leq 14.4$

$k - 4.5 \geq -6.2$

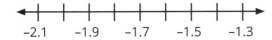

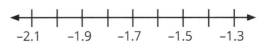

$-7 + u > -12$

$-3.1z < 12.4$

$-2\dfrac{3}{4} > n - 1\dfrac{1}{4}$

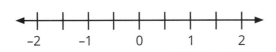

IXL.com
skill ID
TFK

Write an inequality for each problem. Then solve.

A sign for the roller coaster at the county fair states that riders must be at least 36 inches tall to ride. Mandy's little sister is currently 33 inches tall. How many more inches, *n*, does Mandy's little sister need to grow before she can ride the roller coaster?

Mandy's sister needs to grow at least _____ inches.

Isabella is mailing birthday presents for her two cousins. She wants to spend less than $25 to mail the presents. If one package costs $13.25 to ship, how much can the second package cost, *p*?

The second package should cost less than _____.

In Ms. Popa's science class, every student needs at least 30 milliliters of distilled water for an experiment. Ms. Popa has 22 students in her class. How much distilled water, *d*, does she need to order?

Ms. Popa needs to order at least _____ milliliters.

Fred is learning how to roller skate. It takes him $2\frac{1}{2}$ minutes to skate one lap around the rink. Fred sets a goal to skate for more than 30 minutes today. How many laps, *r*, should Fred skate to meet his goal?

Fred should skate more than _____ laps.

Keep going! Write an inequality for each problem. Then solve.

Ted is an avid tennis player and sets a budget for tennis supplies every month. This month, he spent $39.50 on a tennis racket. He knows he can spend up to $20.50 on new tennis balls and still stay within his budget. How much money, *m*, does Ted want to spend on tennis supplies for this month?

Ted wants to spend up to _____ on tennis supplies.

Mr. Dobbs is buying books for his 9 grandchildren. He would like to give each child at least 3 books. How many books, *b*, will Mr. Dobbs buy?

Mr. Dobbs will buy at least _____ books.

Maggie got $65 for her birthday and wants to buy new shoes. Each pair of shoes costs $26. How many pairs of shoes, *s*, can Maggie buy with the birthday money?

Maggie can buy no more than _____ pairs of shoes.

Learn!

You can also use inverse operations to solve inequalities with more than one step. Remember, you must flip the inequality sign if you multiply or divide by a negative number. Try it! Solve $-3x + 5 < 8$. Then graph the solution set on the number line.

$$-3x + 5 < 8$$

$$-3x + 5 - 5 < 8 - 5$$ Subtract 5 from both sides of the inequality. Then simplify.

$$-3x < 3$$

$$\frac{-3x}{-3} > \frac{3}{-3}$$ Divide both sides of the inequality by –3. Then simplify.

$$x > -1$$

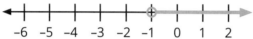

Solve each inequality. Then graph the solution set on the number line.

$$7p - 2 \geq 5$$

$$-4r + 3 < 11$$

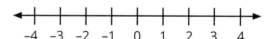

$$1 < -10g - 4$$

$$\frac{x}{2} - 13 \geq -17$$

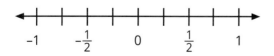

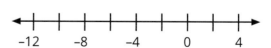

Keep going! Solve each inequality. Then graph the solution set on the number line.

$-5 - 4t \geq -61$

$\dfrac{b}{6} - 4.3 \geq -3.9$

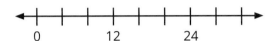

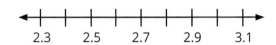

$\dfrac{3}{4}x + 3 \leq -3$

$-29.4 < -7.3h + 14.4$

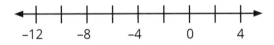

$\dfrac{2}{3}r - 5\dfrac{1}{3} \geq 1\dfrac{1}{3}$

IXL.com
skill ID
XGQ

Draw a line between each inequality and its graphed solution.

$2x + 4.6 > 8.6$

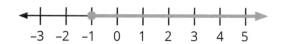

$\dfrac{x}{2} + 10 \leq 9$

$-5x - 13 > -28$

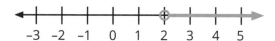

$-\dfrac{2}{3}x + \dfrac{1}{3} \leq 1$

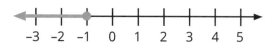

$7x - 6 \leq -13$

IXL.com
skill ID
6TT

Solve each inequality. Then graph the solution set on the number line.

$5(s + 8) \leq 95$

$4x + 3 + 2x - 5 < -14$

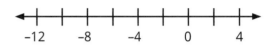

$6(2n - 9) \geq 42$

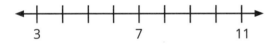

$-28 < -4(r - 9)$

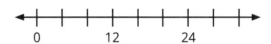

$-6 < 3v + 4 - 8v$

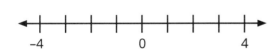

$2(4 + 5w) - 6w - 16 > 2$

Write an inequality for each problem. Then solve.

Mr. Mobley is planning his school's graduation ceremony, and he would like to give each student a small gift from the school. The budget is $500, and he has already spent $140 on caps and gowns. If 50 students are graduating, how much money, g, can Mr. Mobley spend on each gift?

Mr. Mobley can spend up to _____ on each gift.

Ada's piano teacher recommended that she practice at least 5 hours this week to prepare for her concert. She practiced for 3 hours on Sunday. If Ada practices the same amount every day for the next 6 days, how many hours, h, should she practice each day?

Ada should practice at least _____ of an hour each day.

Liam is saving money to buy a new surfboard that costs $130. He deposits $20 in his bank account at the end of every week, but he also wants to have over $50 left in his bank account after the purchase. For how many weeks, w, does Liam need to save?

Liam needs to save for more than _____ weeks.

Pete received a $30 gift card for Purrfect Pet. He buys his cat, Skipper, a toy for $8.50 and wants to buy treats that cost $5 per box. How many boxes of treats, b, can Pete buy without going over $30?

Pete can buy at most _____ boxes of treats.

Keep going! Write an inequality for each problem. Then solve.

Andre baked 60 gingerbread cookies. He wants to give each of his friends the same number of cookies and leave at least 16 for his family. If Andre is sharing the cookies with 9 of his friends, how many cookies, c, can Andre give to each friend?

Andre can give at most _____ cookies to each friend.

At the natural history museum, a yearly family membership costs $65.99 plus an additional $5 for each guest. Ms. Frank wants to spend less than $100 for her family and guests to go to the museum this year. How many guests, g, can her family bring?

They can bring no more than _____ guests.

Lara volunteers a minimum of 4 hours every week at Annie's Animal Sanctuary. First, she spends $1\frac{1}{2}$ hours feeding all the animals. Then, she spends $\frac{1}{4}$ of an hour taking each dog on a walk. How many dogs, d, can Lara walk when she volunteers?

Lara can walk at least _____ dogs.

A **population** is an entire group of people or objects from which data is collected. Statistical questions can help gather information and draw conclusions about a specific population.

Identify the population in each of the statistical questions.

What is the most common color of cars in the Northview Mall parking lot?

Population: ___all of the cars in the Northview Mall parking lot___

Do more customers of Prized Pizza order delivery, order takeout, or eat in the restaurant?

Population: _____

What percentage of seventh-grade students at Brooks Middle School like science fiction movies?

Population: _____

Which graphic novels have the most sales in the Books for You chain of stores?

Population: _____

What is the average price of a laptop in Best Tech stores?

Population: _____

What is the most common occupation of people who work in Watertown?

Population: _____

Learn!

Sometimes collecting data from an entire population can be unrealistic or inefficient. So, you can collect data from a **sample**, or a smaller part of the population.

If a sample has the same characteristics as the population, it is considered a **representative sample**. One way to make sure that a sample is representative is to collect the data in a **random** fashion. This means that every member of the population has an equal chance of being included in the sample. If the sample is not random, the data is likely to be **biased** and not representative of the population.

Answer each question.

Noah wants to know if there is a connection between the number of hours of sleep and time spent playing sports for seventh-grade students at his school. He surveys 10 students from the basketball team. Is the sample likely to be representative?   Yes   No

Hugo is curious as to whether families in his neighborhood have pets. He puts all the addresses in a hat and randomly chooses 25 houses to survey. Is the sample likely to be biased?   Yes   No

Vic wants to know which fruits are most popular for students to eat at lunch. He visits the cafeteria and surveys 30 students from every grade. Is the sample likely to be representative?   Yes   No

Susan wants to know if middle school students who play video games also watch a lot of movies. She surveys 20 middle school students at the Gamer Movie Theater. Is the sample likely to be biased?   Yes   No

Bonnie wonders what percentage of the students at her school like listening to pop music. She surveys 15 students in the school orchestra and another 15 students in the school choir. Is this a random sample?   Yes   No

For more practice, visit IXL.com or the IXL mobile app and enter this code in the search bar.

IXL.com skill ID
5V3

Describe a sampling method that could be used to answer each statistical question. The sampling method should result in a representative sample.

Elizabeth wants to know how much water students in her school typically drink in a day. Describe a sampling method that Elizabeth could use.

Elizabeth could ask every fifth student who walks into the school in the morning.

Jayla wonders how many flavors of ice cream are sold at different ice cream shops in her city. Describe a sampling method that Jayla could use.

Doug wants to know the typical length of a word in his favorite poem. Describe a sampling method that Doug could use.

Ms. Wade is running for mayor of Morrisville and wants to predict her chances of winning. Describe a sampling method that Ms. Wade could use.

The event manager wants to know whether players in the soccer tournament prefer water or sports drinks. Describe a sampling method that the event manager could use.

Exploration Zone

Enrico Fermi was an Italian physicist who was interested in math problems that
we may never know the exact answer to. This kind of math problem is often called
a *Fermi question*. It requires you to make a good estimate with just a little bit of
collected data.

TRY IT YOURSELF!

Answer the Fermi question below.

How many times does an average person's heart beat each day?

Identify the population.

_____

Determine a sample that you could collect data from. Describe how you would collect
the data.

_____

_____

_____

_____

Do you think your sample described above would be a representative sample?
Explain your reasoning.

_____

_____

As an extension, you can collect and record the data from your sample. Then you
can use your data to help you make a conclusion about the Fermi question.

Learn!

When collecting data from a sample, you can use proportions to help you make estimates about the population size. Look at the example.

Scientists in the Arctic tagged 150 walruses in order to study them. Later, the scientists observed a group of 200 walruses and saw that 3 of them were tagged. What is the best estimate of the size of the walrus population?

First, set up the proportion. Plug in the numbers you know and use a variable for the unknown number.

$$\frac{\text{\# of tagged walruses}}{\text{total walrus population}} = \frac{\text{\# of tagged walruses observed}}{\text{total \# of walruses observed}}$$

$$\frac{150}{p} = \frac{3}{200}$$

Next, solve the proportion.

$$150 \cdot 200 = 3p$$

$$\frac{30{,}000}{3} = \frac{3p}{3}$$

So, 10,000 walruses is the best estimate for the size of the population.

$$10{,}000 = p$$

Answer the question.

A researcher for the fishing industry studies the yellow perch population in Lake Holly. She captures and tags 75 fish and releases them back into the lake. Later, the researcher captures 800 fish and finds that only 2 of them are tagged. What is the best estimate of the number of yellow perch in the lake?

_____

Answer each question.

The Springfield Division of Wildlife studied the deer population in a town where the number of deer sightings was increasing. They tagged 15 deer and released them back into the town. Later, they captured 50 deer and found that 5 of them were tagged. What is the best estimate of the number of deer in the town?

_____

Josh was curious what flavor is the most popular for birthday cakes. He visited a local baker and learned that the bakery sold 14 birthday cakes this week, and 8 of those cakes were chocolate. If the bakery sold 70 birthday cakes in the past month, what is the best estimate for the number of cakes that were chocolate?

_____

Mae was curious about the movie genres that her classmates like the best. She surveyed 30 students and found that 15 enjoy adventure movies, 9 like comedies, and 6 prefer dramas. If there are 140 seventh-grade students in Mae's school, what is the best estimate of the number of students who like comedies?

_____

Find the mean, median, mode, and range for each data set.

Avery measured how many inches it snowed each day during one week in December.

1   4   0   0   3   7   6

Mean = _____   Median = _____   Mode = _____   Range = _____

Dillon's family had a garage sale last weekend. He recorded the price of each item sold.

$5 $5 $10 $5 $7 $11 $7 $6

Mean = _____   Median = _____   Mode = _____   Range = _____

Rose measured the height, in centimeters, of all the plants growing in her garden.

94   58   100   75   38   92   60   49   61   83

Mean = _____   Median = _____   Mode = _____   Range = _____

Coach Perry counted the number of raffle tickets that 12 of his players sold.

75   80   83   53   57   78   64   73   59   63   72   83

Mean = _____   Median = _____   Mode = _____   Range = _____

IXL.com
skill ID
U2A

The **mean absolute deviation (MAD)** is a number that measures the variability of a data set, or how spread out the data values are from the mean.

Try it! Calculate the MAD for each data set. Find the distance each data point is from the mean. Then, find the mean of those distances.

10   8   11   12   6   13

MAD = _____

2   5   2   4   7

MAD = _____

20   27   4   21   28

MAD = _____

31   43   26   52   33   47   34

MAD = _____

16   18   12   20   19   11

MAD = _____

67   70   82   78   65   78   80   64

MAD = _____

Measures of center and measures of variation can be used to draw inferences about a data set. Answer each question.

Terry recorded the number of pets that each student in his class has.

Number of pets	Frequency
0	2
1	4
2	7
3	4
4	2

What is the mean of this data set?

_____

What is the range of this data set?

_____

Terry infers that students in his class generally have 2 pets. Do you agree? Why or why not?

_____

_____

Carlos recorded the high temperature for the first 15 days in May.

High temperature (°F)		
65	71	67
74	75	73
68	72	73
76	74	65
78	80	70

What is the median of this data set?

_____

What is the range of this data set?

_____

Carlos infers that the high temperature is generally above 75°F. Do you agree? Why or why not?

_____

_____

Measures of center and measures of variation can also be used to compare data. Answer each question.

A group of students compared their high scores in the video games *Dance Depot* and *Rhythm Rhymes*. The maximum possible score in each game is 100 points.

High scores in *Dance Depot*		
90	82	56
79	100	98
85	93	72
67	81	99

High scores in *Rhythm Rhymes*		
34	55	84
61	42	51
74	27	100
55	63	79

Which game has a smaller range of high scores? _____

Which game has a lower median high score? _____

Which game would you infer generally has higher scores? _____

Dr. Hill recorded the weight of each dog and cat that came into her office on Tuesday.

Weight of dogs (lb.)		
15	8	23
54	86	37
49	62	28

Weight of cats (lb.)		
8	11	9
10	9	13
7	10	11

Which animal's weight has a larger range? _____

Which animal's weight has a smaller mean? _____

Which animal's weight would you infer is more variable? _____

Each member of the Rolesville robotics team built a remote-controlled robot and recorded how many seconds it took the robot to complete an obstacle course.

Create a dot plot of the data.

Time (seconds)				
10	20	16	17	18
12	11	12	15	12
19	16	11	12	10
17	12	15	11	14

Robots' travel time

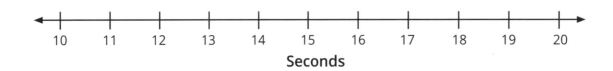

Seconds

Use the dot plot to fill in the blanks.

_____ seconds was the most common time it took the robots to complete the obstacle course.

On average, the robots took _____ seconds to complete the obstacle course.

Answer each question.

A group of contestants displayed their accuracy in archery and basketball. Each had 10 tries to hit a target in the archery event and 10 tries to make a basket in the basketball event.

Archery event

Number of targets hit

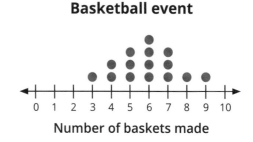

Basketball event

Number of baskets made

Which event has a higher median? _____

Which event's data set is more symmetrical? _____

Which event would you infer is more variable? _____

Gabriella asked the students in her homeroom how many times they visited the movie theater and the park last month.

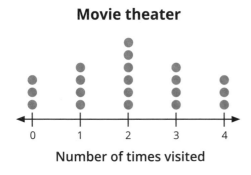

Movie theater

Number of times visited

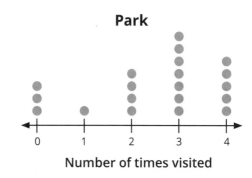

Park

Number of times visited

Which location has a higher mean? _____

Which location's data set is more symmetrical? _____

Which location would you infer more students generally visit?

_____

IXL.com
skill ID
W92

Vivian asked 16 members of the Blue Ridge Marching Band how many hours they spent practicing their instrument last week.

Create a box plot of the data.

Hours spent practicing last week			
9	0	4	6
4	5	3	8
10	4	6	7
7	2	7	6

Time spent practicing last week

Hours

Use the box plot to fill in the blanks.

_____% of the members practiced less than 4 hours last week.

Half of the members practiced more than _____ hours last week.

Answer each question.

Paola is deciding which cell phone to purchase. Paola compared the battery life of cell phones from two different brands: Planet Phone and Moon Mobile.

Battery life of cell phones

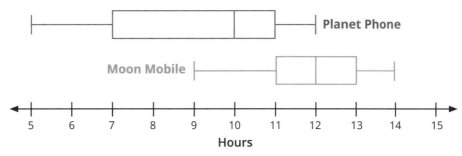

Which brand has a greater IQR (interquartile range)? _____

Which brand's data set is more symmetrical? _____

Which brand would you infer has phones with longer battery life? _____

Aria's garden is filled with her two favorite types of flowers: sunflowers and foxgloves. She measured the height of each flower in her garden.

Height of flowers

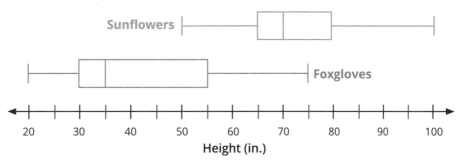

Which type of flower has a greater range? _____

Which type of flower's data set is more symmetrical? _____

Which type of flower would you infer is generally shorter?

_____

Learn!

Probability is a measure of how likely an event is to occur. Probability can be measured using numbers from 0 to 1. A probability that is closer to 0 means an event is less likely to happen. A probability that is closer to 1 means an event is more likely to happen.

The probability of a simple event can be written as the ratio of the favorable outcomes to the total number of possible outcomes. You can write this as a fraction, decimal, or percent.

$$\text{Probability} = \frac{\text{number of favorable outcomes}}{\text{total number of possible outcomes}}$$

Try it! Olivia rolls a 6-sided die. What is the probability that she will roll an odd number?

$P(\text{odd}) = \frac{3}{6} = \frac{1}{2} = 0.5 = 50\%$ A 6-sided die has 6 numbers, 3 of which are odd. So, the probability that Olivia will roll an odd number is $\frac{1}{2}$ or 50%.

Find each probability.

Noah picks a number at random.

3 4
5 6

$P(4) =$ _____

$P(> 6) =$ _____

$P(\text{multiple of 3}) =$ _____

Maya randomly chooses a podcast to listen to out of her top 5 podcasts. Of those podcasts, 3 of the hosts are celebrities, 1 is an athlete, and 1 is a journalist.

$P(\text{celebrity}) =$ _____

$P(\text{journalist}) =$ _____

$P(\text{not a journalist}) =$ _____

IXL.com
skill ID
ZZB

Keep going! Find each probability.

Oliver chooses a shape at random.

$P(\geq 3 \text{ sides}) = $ _____

$P(\text{square}) = $ _____

$P(\text{equilateral triangle}) = $ _____

Emma spins the spinner.

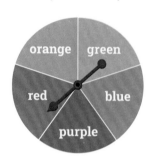

$P(\text{purple}) = $ _____

$P(\text{orange or blue}) = $ _____

$P(\text{yellow}) = $ _____

Charlotte picks a card at random.

| 6 | 25 | 100 | 20 | 2,000 |
| 1,000 | 80 | 10 | 660 | 7 |

$P(< 1{,}000) = $ _____

$P(\text{prime}) = $ _____

$P(\text{not 2 digits}) = $ _____

THINK ABOUT IT! Go back and find one probability on this page that could be considered likely and one probability that could be considered unlikely.

Use the spinner to find the path from start to finish. If the probability is less than 50%, move one space to the left. If the probability is greater than 50%, move one space to the right. If the probability is equal to 50%, move one space down.

START

P(3 or 7)	P(even number)	P(5)	P(> 2)	P(not a factor of 6)
P(not even)	P(multiple of 3)	P(not 6 or 7)	P(factor of 5)	P(> 8)
P(factor of 6)	P(≥ 9)	P(factor of 16)	P(0)	P(odd number)
P(less than 10)	P(not a multiple of 4)	P(> 3)	P(not < 5)	P(1)
P(not 4)	P(> 1)	P(not 2 or 3)	P(not 1)	P(multiple of 2)

FINISH

Learn!

You can use probability to make predictions. Look at the example.

If 300 people randomly choose a number from 1 to 5, what is the best prediction for the number of people who choose 4?

$$\frac{1}{5} = \frac{x}{300}$$ Set up a proportion. For the first ratio, the probability of choosing a 4 is $\frac{1}{5}$. For the second ratio, the number of people who choose 4 is unknown. Write a variable, x, over the total number of people, which is 300.

$$300 = 5x$$ Solve the proportion.

$$\frac{300}{5} = \frac{5x}{5}$$

$$60 = x$$ So, the best prediction is that 60 people choose the number 4.

Use probability to make each prediction.

If Amelia flips a coin 90 times, what is the best prediction for the number of times it will land on heads? _____

If James rolls a 6-sided die 36 times, what is the best prediction for the number of times he will roll a number greater than 4? _____

There are 5 blue marbles and 3 orange marbles in a bag. William randomly selects a marble and puts it back in the bag. If he does this 40 times, what is the best prediction for the number of times William will pick a blue marble? _____

IXL.com
skill ID

9UW

Learn!

Experimental probability is a probability that is based on collected data. It can be expressed as the ratio of the number of times a result occurs to the total number of trials.

$$\text{Experimental probability} = \frac{\text{number of times a result occurs}}{\text{total number of trials}}$$

Try it! Lucas flips a coin 50 times and lands on tails 30 of those times. Find the experimental probability that Lucas lands on tails.

$$\frac{30}{50} = \frac{3}{5} = 0.6 = 60\%$$

So, the experimental probability that Lucas lands on tails is $\frac{3}{5}$ or 60%.

Find each experimental probability.

At the seventh grade celebration, 4 of the first 10 students asked for sprinkles on their ice cream sundaes. What is the experimental probability that the next student asks for sprinkles?

P(sprinkles) =_____

Marco has taken 8 penalty shots, and 6 of his shots resulted in goals. What is the experimental probability that Marco scores a goal on a penalty shot?

P(goal) = _____

Shivani has been trying to improve her score in *Warriors of the World*. In the past 10 games, she scored over 2,000 points 8 different times. What is the experimental probability that Shivani will score over 2,000 points in the next game she plays?

P(> 2,000 points) = _____

Of the 16 birds that came to the bird feeder this morning, 2 were robins. What is the experimental probability that the next bird to come to the bird feeder will be a robin?

P(robin) = _____

Keep going! Find each experimental probability.

Valerie asked her friends how many hours they listen to music each week. What is the experimental probability that the next friend Valerie asks listens to music 5 hours per week?

Number of hours	2	3	4	5	6
Number of friends	1	0	3	4	12

$P(5 \text{ hours}) = $ _____

Musically Yours tracked recent sales of each type of instrument. What is the experimental probability that the next instrument sold is a guitar?

Instrument	piano	guitar	flute	drums	cello
Number sold	13	15	4	12	6

$P(\text{guitar}) = $ _____

Mr. Lee asked some of his students about their favorite after-school activity. What is the experimental probability that the next student he asks participates in art?

Activity	sports	drama	music	art	coding
Number of students	8	5	6	7	2

$P(\text{art}) = $ _____

Learn!

You can also use experimental probability to make predictions. Look at the example.

Harper has successfully solved a word puzzle 3 times in the last 5 tries. Based on this data, how many word puzzles can Harper expect to solve out of the next 30 tries?

$$\frac{3}{5} = \frac{n}{30}$$ Write a proportion that sets the two ratios equal to each other.

$$3 \cdot 30 = 5n$$ Solve the proportion.

$$\frac{90}{5} = \frac{5n}{5}$$

$$18 = n$$ So, Harper can expect to solve 18 word puzzles out of the next 30 puzzles she tries.

Use experimental probability to make each prediction.

Students in the nature club are observing insects in their school garden. Yesterday they counted 8 insects, 3 of which were varieties of beetles. Based on this data, how many of the next 48 insects would they expect to be beetles?   —————————

The owner of Bowling Bonanza noted that 5 of the last 12 customers brought their own bowling ball. Based on this data, how many of the next 60 customers would the owner expect to bring their own bowling ball?   —————————

This month, the park ranger saw a brown bear 2 times in 30 days. Based on this data, how many times in the next 90 days would the park ranger expect to see a brown bear?   —————————

IXL.com
skill ID
WP6

Keep going! Use experimental probability to make each prediction.

Colin is working to increase his typing speed. Based on the data in the table, how many times should Colin expect to type 37 words per minute out of the next 10 times he types?

Words per minute	20	28	32	37
Number of times	3	3	6	8

_____

Frieda asked a group of people how many times they went to the beach last summer. Based on the data in the table, how many people would Frieda expect to have gone to the beach 2 times if she asks 35 people?

Number of times	1	2	3	4
Number of people	6	2	5	1

_____

A tailor has a collection of buttons in a jar. She pulled out a handful and recorded the data in a table. Based on this data, about how many fabric buttons would the tailor expect to have in a jar of 100 buttons?

Type of button	wood	fabric	plastic	metal
Number of buttons	5	3	5	2

_____

IXL.com
skill ID
VST

> **Learn!**
>
> When all outcomes of an experiment are equally likely, the event has **uniform probability**. For example, a standard 6-sided die has 6 sides, each with a different number. It is equally likely that any of the sides will be on top after rolling the die. So, the probability of rolling a 1, 2, 3, 4, 5, or 6 is always $\frac{1}{6}$.

Determine if each situation describes a uniform probability model.

Theo spins the spinner.

uniform   not uniform

Evie randomly chooses a number.

uniform   not uniform

Brayden randomly places a piece on the gameboard.

uniform   not uniform

Tisha reaches into a bag without looking and grabs a shape.

uniform   not uniform

Create a uniform probability model for each problem.

Draw a spinner that has an equal chance of spinning the letters in the word SPIN.

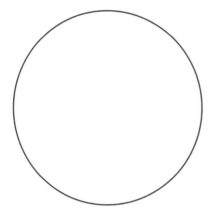

Number the cards so there is an equal chance of getting a positive number or a negative number.

Design the circles so there is an equal chance of choosing a white or patterned circle.

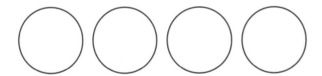

Write a first name so that all the letters in the name have an equal chance of being randomly picked.

_____

Learn!

The **sample space** of an event is the set of all possible outcomes. You can use a tree diagram, a table, or an organized list to show the set of all possible outcomes of a **compound event**, which consists of two or more events.

Try it! Find the sample space of choosing a card and spinning the spinner. The card can be 3, 4, 5, or 6. The spinner can land on orange (O) or green (G).

| | Tree diagram | | Table | | | | | Organized list |

Tree diagram

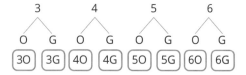

Table

	3	4	5	6
orange	3O	4O	5O	6O
green	3G	4G	5G	6G

Organized list

3O, 3G
4O, 4G
5O, 5G
6O, 6G

The tree diagram, table, and organized list all show that there are **8 possible outcomes** in the sample space.

Use a tree diagram, table, or organized list to find the sample space. Then write the number of possible outcomes.

Find the sample space of flipping a coin and spinning the spinner below.

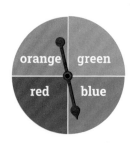

There are _____ possible outcomes in the sample space.

Keep going! Use a tree diagram, table, or organized list to find the sample space. Then write the number of possible outcomes.

Find the sample space of rolling a 6-sided die and flipping a coin.

There are _____ possible outcomes in the sample space.

Find the sample space of rolling a 6-sided die and spinning the spinner below.

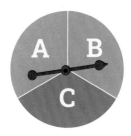

There are _____ possible outcomes in the sample space.

Find the sample space of flipping three coins.

There are _____ possible outcomes in the sample space.

Learn!

Another way to find the total number of possible outcomes of compound events is to use the **fundamental counting principle**. It says you can multiply the number of choices in each event to find the total number of outcomes. Look at the example.

Sarah is deciding on her outfit for the day. She is choosing from 4 different shirts and 3 different pairs of pants. How many different outfits can Sarah make?

4 × 3 = 12   Sarah can make 12 different outfits.

Determine the total number of possible outcomes.

Next semester, Sue can select one of 5 foreign language electives and one of 3 music electives. How many different combinations can Sue select?

_____

Tessa is ordering lunch with one appetizer and one entree. The appetizer choices are salad, vegetable soup, or fruit cup. The entree choices are hamburger, chicken sandwich, or veggie burger. How many different lunches can Tessa order?

_____

Antonio is attending the winter concert at his school and wants to order snacks during intermission. The snack stand has 4 types of chips, 4 varieties of cookies, and 2 different drinks to choose from. If Antonio wants to buy one of each item, how many different combinations can he buy?

_____

Jeff is making an omelet. There are 3 types of meat, 4 types of cheese, and 4 vegetables to choose from. How many different omelets can Jeff make using exactly one of each item?

_____

IXL.com
skill ID
EKX

Learn!

You can find the **probability of compound events** in the same way you find the probability of simple events.

$$\text{Probability} = \frac{\text{number of favorable outcomes}}{\text{number of outcomes in the sample space}}$$

Try it! If Hallie flips a coin and rolls a 6-sided die, what is the probability she will land on heads and roll an even number?

2 × 6 = 12	There are 2 outcomes when flipping a coin and 6 outcomes when rolling a 6-sided die. So, there are 12 possible outcomes in the sample space.
1 × 3 = 3	There is 1 side of a coin that is heads and 3 even numbers on a 6-sided die. So, there are 3 ways to land on heads and roll an even number.
$\frac{3}{12} = \frac{1}{4}$	So, the probability is $\frac{1}{4}$ or 25%.

Find each probability.

David spins the spinner below twice. What is the probability that he lands on blue both times?   _____

Mia flips a coin and randomly picks a card below. What is the probability of landing on tails and picking a number less than 5?   _____

3 4 5 6 7

Keep going! Find each probability.

Janet Chang randomly chooses one letter from her first name and one letter from her last name. What is the probability that she chooses her initials, JC?

_____

Marcus has the two bags of tiles below. If he randomly chooses one tile from each bag, what is the probability that Marcus picks a vowel and a multiple of 2?

_____

Rachel spins each of the spinners below. What is the probability that Rachel lands on a consonant and a number greater than 1?

_____

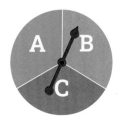 

Jacob rolls a 6-sided die two times. What is the probability that he rolls two even numbers?

_____

Answer each question.

The Drake family is playing a game where each player spins the two spinners below. What is the probability that the next person will land on green and a point value greater than 2?

Ms. Bales is making snack bags for each student going on a field trip. She randomly places one food item and one drink in each bag. There is an equal chance of the food item being a granola bar, a bag of chips, an apple, a banana, or an orange. There is an equal chance that the drink is orange juice, apple juice, water, or tea. What is the probability that a student will get a snack bag with a food item that is a fruit and a drink that is not fruit juice?

Exploration Zone

A **simulation** is an experiment that represents a real-world situation. A simulation can help you estimate real-world probabilities. You can run a simulation many times to find an experimental probability.

TRY IT YOURSELF!

Jamie's cat is having kittens! The veterinarian said that Jamie's cat will have four kittens, and each kitten will have either black or brown fur. There is an equal chance that a kitten will have either color fur. Jamie wants to know how likely it is that at least three of the kittens will have black fur.

What is the probability of one of the kittens having black fur? _____

Design a simulation that uses coins to determine the probability of Jamie's cat having at least three kittens with black fur.

Explain how you could use coins to simulate the color of each kitten's fur.

_____

_____

_____

Explain how you would run each trial of your simulation.

_____

_____

_____

_____

Run the simulation you designed using coins. Run 20 trials. Record your data in the table below.

Trial 1	Trial 2	Trial 3	Trial 4
Trial 5	Trial 6	Trial 7	Trial 8
Trial 9	Trial 10	Trial 11	Trial 12
Trial 13	Trial 14	Trial 15	Trial 16
Trial 17	Trial 18	Trial 19	Trial 20

Based on your simulation, what is the probability that Jamie's cat will have at least three kittens with black fur? _____

Learn!

Compound events can be **independent** or **dependent**. For independent events, the outcome of the first event does *not* affect the outcome of the next event. For dependent events, the outcome of the first event does affect the outcome of the next event. Look at the example.

All of the letters of the word PROBABILITY are placed in a bag. Without looking, Raj selects one letter from the bag and does not replace it. He then randomly selects a second letter from the bag. These events are dependent because Raj's first choice affects the possible outcomes for his second choice. Raj will have one less letter to choose from.

Determine if the events are independent or dependent.

Without looking, Meg chooses a colored marble from a bag, writes down the color, and returns it to the bag. Then, she draws another marble without looking.

independent

Ms. Daniels has 20 numbered boxes, and each box has a prize inside. First, Jerry randomly chooses a numbered box and keeps the prize. Then, Monica randomly chooses one of the remaining numbered boxes.

_____

Jasmine randomly chooses a queen from a deck of cards. Without replacing it, she chooses a second card.

_____

Jake is flipping two coins. He flips the first coin. Then he flips the second coin.

_____

Students are playing basketball in gym class. Without looking, Daphne pulls out a yellow jersey from the bag and puts it on. Then Jose pulls out a red jersey from the same bag without looking.

_____

IXL.com
skill ID
9M6

Learn!

To find the probability of dependent events, find the probability of the first event and multiply it by the probability of the second event. Remember that the first event will affect the second event. Look at the example.

Without looking, Jon picks a card from the first group below. Then, without replacing it, he picks another card. What is the probability of Jon picking a 7 and then a 5?

For the first event, the probability of picking a 7 is $\frac{1}{5}$.

After the 7 was picked, the probability of picking a 5 for the second event is $\frac{1}{4}$.

Now, multiply the probability of the first event by the probability of the second event.

$$\frac{1}{5} \times \frac{1}{4} = \frac{1}{20}$$

So, the probability of Jon picking a 7 and then a 5 is $\frac{1}{20}$ or 5%.

Find each probability.

4 2 14 8 10 20   Carol picks a card at random. Without putting the card back, she picks a second card. What is the probability of Carol first picking a 10 and then a number less than 10?

_____

The reading club is randomly choosing the order of the books they will read this year from a list of 5 books. There is a mystery and a biography on the list. What is the probability that the first book is the mystery and the second book is not the biography?

_____

Raina has a bag with 4 red marbles and 1 green marble. She picks a marble at random. Then, without putting it back, she picks a second marble at random. What is the probability of picking a green marble and then picking another green marble?

_____

IXL.com
skill ID
NED

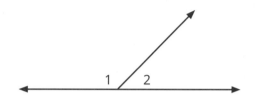

Learn!

Complementary angles have a sum of 90°.

∠1 and ∠2 are complementary angles.

Supplementary angles have a sum of 180°.

∠1 and ∠2 are supplementary angles.

Vertical angles are a pair of opposite angles that form when two lines intersect. Vertical angles are congruent.

∠1 and ∠4 are vertical angles.
Also, ∠2 and ∠3 are vertical angles.

Adjacent angles share a common **vertex** and **side**.

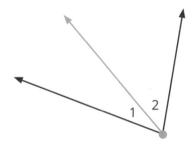

∠1 and ∠2 are adjacent angles.

Answer each question.

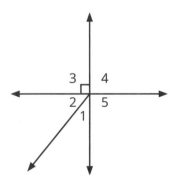

Which angle is complementary to ∠2? _____

Name an angle that is supplementary to ∠3. _____

∠5 and _____ are a pair of vertical angles.

Keep going! Answer each question.

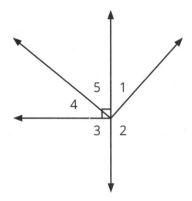

Which angle is adjacent to ∠3, other than ∠4? _____

Which angle is complementary to ∠5? _____

Name the angle that is supplementary to ∠2. _____

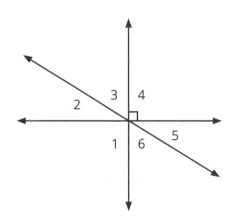

Name an angle that is complementary to ∠3. _____

Name the angle that is vertical to ∠4. _____

Name two angles that are adjacent to ∠5.

_____ and _____

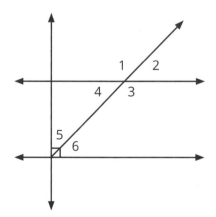

∠4 and _____ are a pair of vertical angles.

Name the angle that is adjacent to ∠5. _____

Which angle is supplementary to ∠3,

other than ∠4? _____

Use angle relationships to find the value of each variable.

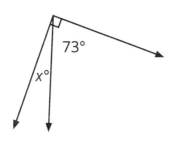

x = _____

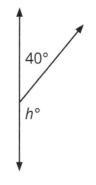

h = _____

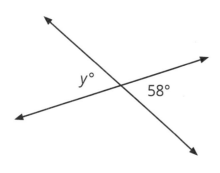

y = _____

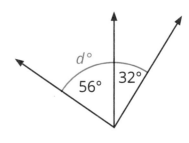

d = _____

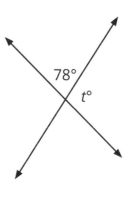

t = _____

Keep going! Use angle relationships to find the value of each variable.

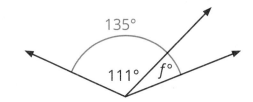

f = _____

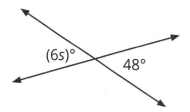

s = _____

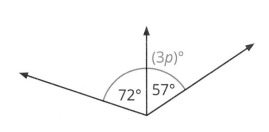

p = _____

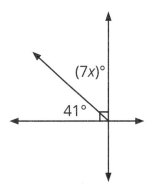

x = _____

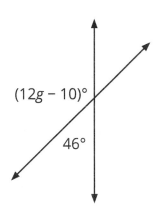

g = _____

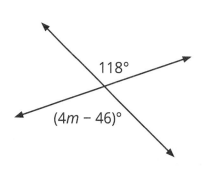

m = _____

Keep going! Use angle relationships to find the value of each variable.

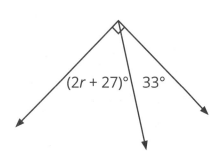

$r =$ _____

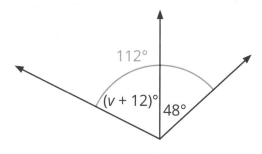

$v =$ _____

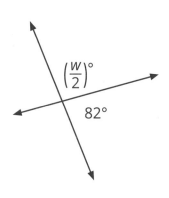

$w =$ _____

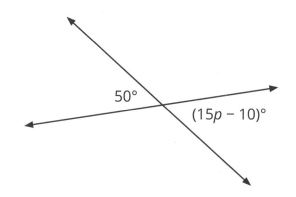

$p =$ _____

Answer each question.

∠QRS is complementary to ∠SRT. The measure of ∠QRS is 42°.
What is the measure of ∠SRT?

_____

∠MNP and ∠PNQ are supplementary. The measure of ∠MNP
is 99°. What is the measure of ∠PNQ?

_____

∠ABC and ∠DBF are vertical angles. The sum of their measures
is 114°. What is the measure of ∠ABC?

_____

∠XYZ measures 10 degrees more than its supplementary angle,
∠WYX. What is the measure of ∠WYX?

_____

∠GHJ and ∠FHJ are adjacent. The measure of ∠GHJ is 24 degrees
less than the measure of ∠FHJ. The sum of their measures is
176°. What is the measure of ∠GHJ?

_____

IXL.com
skill ID
CST

Use angle relationships to find the value of each variable.

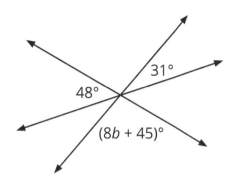

31°

48°

(8b + 45)°

b = _____

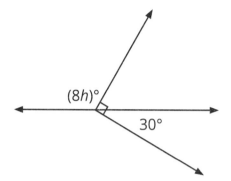

(8h)°

30°

h = _____

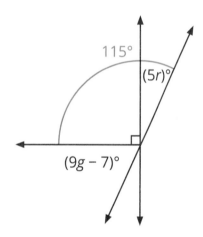

115°

(5r)°

(9g − 7)°

r = _____

g = _____

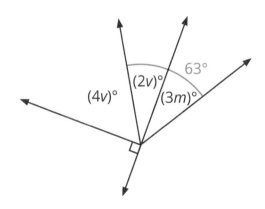

63°

(2v)°

(4v)°

(3m)°

v = _____

m = _____

Use your knowledge of angle relationships to help you answer each question.

In the figure below, line *a* is parallel to line *b*.

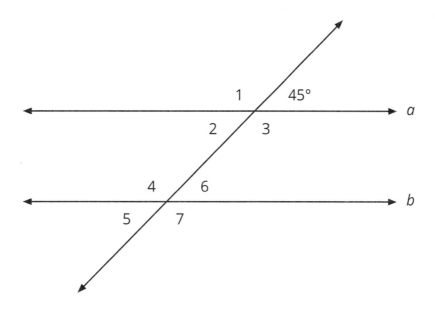

Use the given angle to find the measures of ∠1, ∠2, and ∠3.

m∠1 = _____   m∠2 = _____   m∠3 = _____

Predict the measure of ∠6. _____

Find the actual measure of ∠6. Use a protractor, tracing paper, or another tool to help you.   m∠6 = _____

Now, use the measure of ∠6 to find the measures of ∠4, ∠5, and ∠7.

m∠4 = _____   m∠5 = _____   m∠7 = _____

Which angles in the figure are congruent? _____

_____

In any triangle, the sum of the three interior angles equals 180°. Determine if each of the three given angles forms a triangle.

90° 45° 45°	120° 34° 36°	30° 60° 90°
90° + 45° + 45° = 180°		
(Yes) No	Yes No	Yes No
164° 7° 7°	54° 59° 67°	25° 25° 125°
Yes No	Yes No	Yes No
27° 61° 92°	82.5° 81° 16.5°	89° 24° 57°
Yes No	Yes No	Yes No
113.7° 30.3° 46°	17° 17° 146°	58.9° 60° 61.1°
Yes No	Yes No	Yes No

Find the missing angle measure in each triangle.

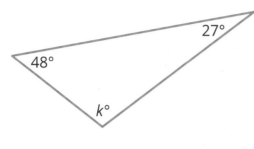

k = _____

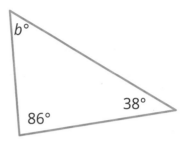

b = _____

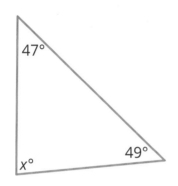

x = _____

p = _____

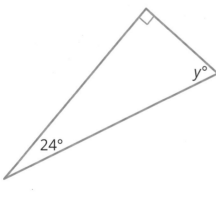

y = _____

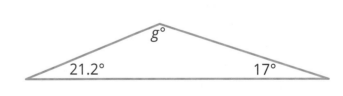

g = _____

For more practice, visit IXL.com or the IXL mobile app and enter this code in the search bar.

IXL.com
skill ID
4U6

Find the value of each variable.

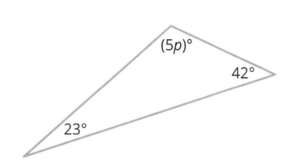

$(5p)°$

$42°$

$23°$

$p = $ _____

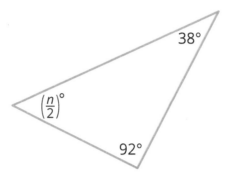

$38°$

$\left(\frac{n}{2}\right)°$

$92°$

$n = $ _____

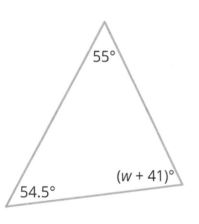

$55°$

$(w + 41)°$

$54.5°$

$w = $ _____

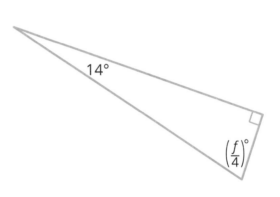

$14°$

$\left(\frac{f}{4}\right)°$

$f = $ _____

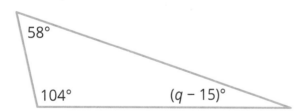

$58°$

$104°$

$(q - 15)°$

$q = $ _____

$37.4°$

$22.6°$

$(3t)°$

$t = $ _____

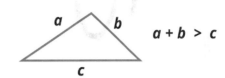

Learn!

In any triangle, the sum of the two shortest side lengths must be greater than the length of the third side.

$a + b > c$

Determine if a triangle can be made with the given side lengths.

3 cm, 4 cm, and 5 cm

$3 + 4 > 5$

(Yes)   No

5 in., 7 in., and 10 in.

Yes   No

4 mm, 6 mm, and 13 mm

Yes   No

14 ft., 14 ft., and 28 ft.

Yes   No

18 mi., 30 mi., and 42 mi.

Yes   No

13 km, 34 km, and 47 km

Yes   No

8.9 cm, 24.1 cm, and 38 cm

Yes   No

8.2 in., 14.7 in., and 19.5 in.

Yes   No

Determine if you can make one triangle, more than one triangle, or no triangle for each description.

A triangle with angle measures of 65°, 40°, and 75° more than one triangle	A triangle with side lengths of 5 cm, 8 cm, and 10 cm
A triangle with angle measures of 52°, 100°, and 28°	A triangle with side lengths of 7 in., 12 in., and 22 in.
A triangle with side lengths of 7 m, 7 m, and 14 m	A triangle with angle measures of 90°, 13.2°, and 76.8°
A triangle with a side length of 7 m between two angles measuring 60° and 40°	A triangle with one side length of 16 mm and one angle measure of 75°

Answer each question.

Edwin painted a picture of a castle with a triangular flag at the top. Using his protractor, he found that two of the angles in the triangle both measured 80°. What was the measure of the third angle?

_____

Mae ordered a custom triangular frame from Simon's Sign Shop. The frame maker at the shop currently has 3 pieces of wood measuring 1 foot, 5 feet, and 3 feet. Will he be able to make a triangle frame for Mae without cutting any of the wood pieces?

_____

Cora wants to build a playpen for her new puppy out of three pieces of fencing. Can Cora build a triangular playpen that has a right angle and an obtuse angle?

_____

Roxanne is making a triangle pendant for her necklace. She has one metal wire that is 32 millimeters long and another that is 22 millimeters long. What are two possible lengths for the third metal wire?

_____

_____

Sketch a polygon for each description below.

A scalene triangle	A quadrilateral with four congruent angles
A quadrilateral with exactly one right angle	A triangle with two acute angles
An isosceles triangle with three acute angles	A parallelogram with two acute angles and two obtuse angles

Keep going! Sketch a polygon for each description below.

An obtuse isosceles triangle	A right scalene triangle
A quadrilateral with two pairs of congruent sides	**A rhombus with at least one right angle**

Get ahead of the curve with extra math practice! Join IXL today.

Scan this QR code for details.

Learn!

A **circle** is a shape made out of points that are all the same distance from a point called the **center**. The **radius**, *r*, is a line segment that connects a point on the circle to the center. The **diameter**, *d*, is a line segment that connects two points on the circle and passes through the center. You can use these formulas to find the length of the diameter or radius.

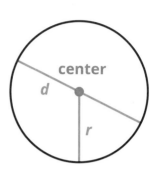

$d = 2r$ The diameter is twice as long as the radius.

$r = \dfrac{d}{2}$ The radius is half the length of the diameter.

Find the diameter or radius of each circle.

 $d =$ _____

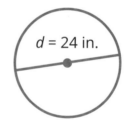 $r =$ _____

 $d =$ _____

 $r =$ _____

IXL.com
skill ID
2VL

 $d =$ _____

Learn!

The **circumference** of a circle is the distance around it, or its perimeter. You can find the circumference using either the diameter or the radius of a circle.

If you know the diameter, d, of a circle, use this formula to find the circumference:

$$C = \pi d$$

If you know the radius, r, of a circle, use this formula to find the circumference:

$$C = 2\pi r$$

Try it! Find the circumference of each circle. You can use 3.14 as an approximation for π.

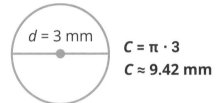

d = 3 mm

$C = \pi \cdot 3$
$C \approx 9.42$ mm

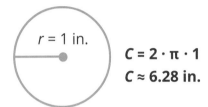

r = 1 in.

$C = 2 \cdot \pi \cdot 1$
$C \approx 6.28$ in.

Find the circumference of each circle. If necessary, round your answer to the nearest hundredth.

d = 10 ft.

$C \approx$ _____

r = 2 cm

$C \approx$ _____

r = 15 in.

$C \approx$ _____

d = 6 mi.

$C \approx$ _____

d = 5.5 m

$C \approx$ _____

r = 2.5 yd.

$C \approx$ _____

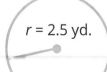

Answer each question. If necessary, round your answer to the nearest hundredth.

The diameter of a circle is 2 millimeters. What is the circle's circumference?

_____

The radius of a circle is 5 yards. What is the circle's circumference?

_____

The circumference of a circle is approximately 25.12 inches. What is the circle's diameter?

_____

The circumference of a circle is approximately 43.96 kilometers. What is the circle's radius?

_____

The radius of a circle is 4.5 centimeters. What is the circle's circumference?

_____

The circumference of a circle is approximately 20.41 meters. What is the circle's diameter?

_____

IXL.com
skill ID
KS7

> ### Learn!
>
> To find the area of a circle with radius r, use the formula $\boldsymbol{A = \pi r^2}$. Try it! Find the area of the circle below. You can use 3.14 as an approximation for π.
>
>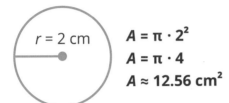
>
> $r = 2$ cm
>
> $\boldsymbol{A = \pi \cdot 2^2}$
> $\boldsymbol{A = \pi \cdot 4}$
> $\boldsymbol{A \approx 12.56}$ cm^2
>
> **Be careful!** If you are given the diameter, you must find the radius before using the formula.

Find the area of each circle. If necessary, round your answer to the nearest hundredth.

$r = 3$ km

$A \approx$ _____

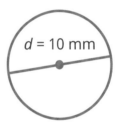

$d = 10$ mm

$A \approx$ _____

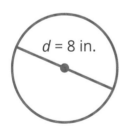

$d = 8$ in.

$A \approx$ _____

$r = 6$ ft.

$A \approx$ _____

$r = 11$ mi.

$A \approx$ _____

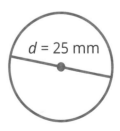

$d = 25$ mm

$A \approx$ _____

Answer each question. If necessary, round your answer to the nearest hundredth.

The radius of a circle is 7 feet. What is the circle's area?

_____

The diameter of a circle is 4 meters. What is the circle's area?

_____

The diameter of a circle is 16 inches. What is the circle's area?

_____

The radius of a circle is 3.5 meters. What is the circle's area?

_____

The diameter of a circle is 27 yards. What is the circle's area?

_____

IXL.com
skill ID
YA8

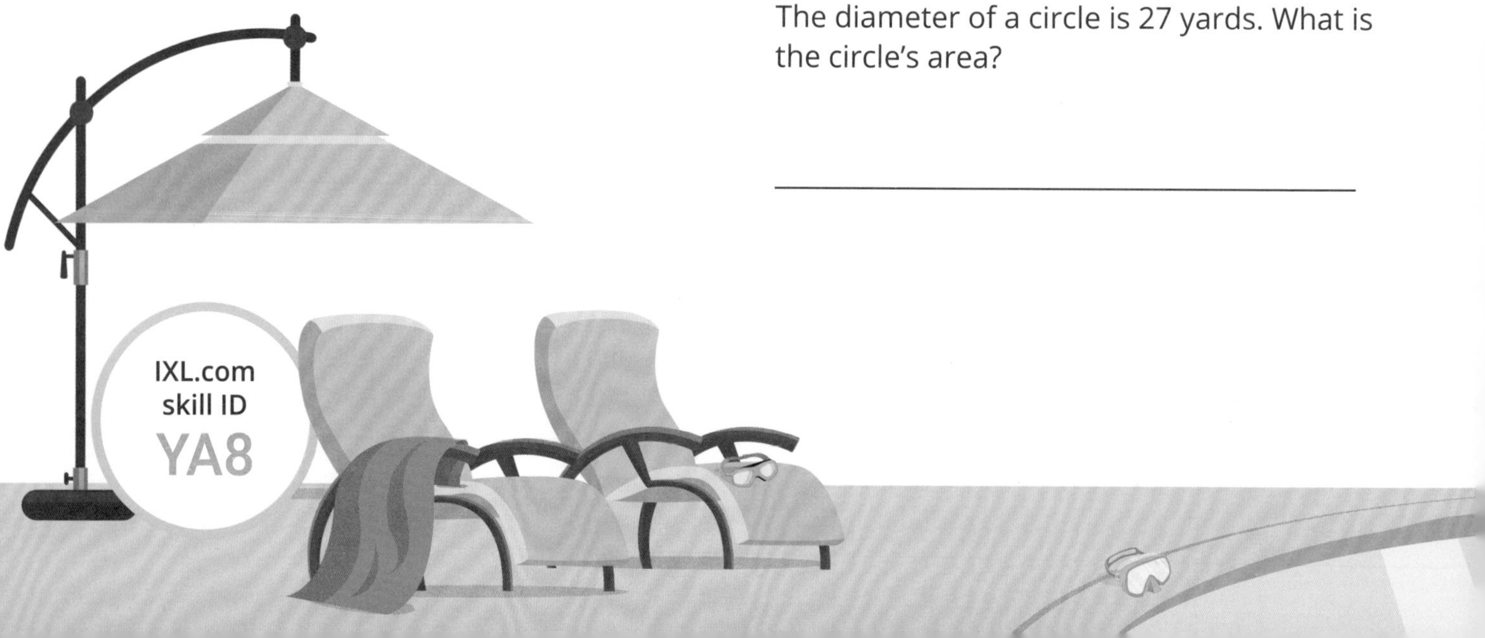

Answer each question. If necessary, round your answer to the nearest hundredth.

Russell ordered a medium pizza from Roni's Pizza Parlor, and the pizza has a diameter of 12 inches. What is the area of the pizza?

_____

Pedro has a circular pool in his backyard with a radius of 6 meters. What is the approximate distance around the edge of Pedro's pool?

_____

There is a clock tower at the center of Elmwood Square. The minute hand measures 3 meters long, and it extends from the center to the edge of the clock face. What is the area of the clock face?

_____

A gardener wants to plant a seed so that a tomato plant grows exactly in the center of a pot. He knows the circumference of the pot is approximately 81.64 centimeters. How far from the edge of the pot should the gardener plant the seed?

_____

Dani's unicycle wheel has a radius of 1.2 feet. How far will Dani's unicycle travel after one rotation of the wheel?

_____

Exploration Zone

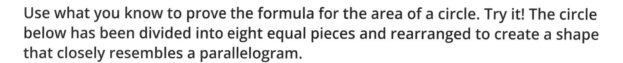

Use what you know to prove the formula for the area of a circle. Try it! The circle below has been divided into eight equal pieces and rearranged to create a shape that closely resembles a parallelogram.

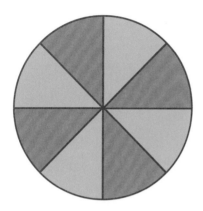 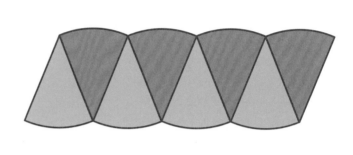

How do the areas of the two shapes compare? _____

_____

The same circle has been divided into sixteen equal pieces and rearranged to create a shape that *even more closely* resembles a parallelogram.

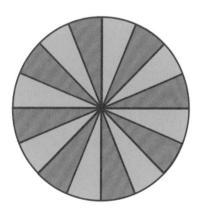 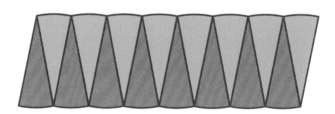

How do the areas of the two shapes compare? _____

_____

If you continue cutting the circle into even smaller pieces and rearranging them, the shape would continue looking *even more and more* like a parallelogram.

Use the diagram to answer each question.

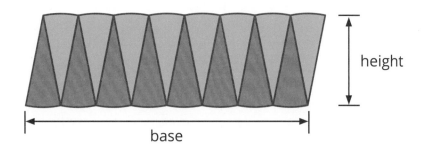

base

height

1. The base of the shape is approximately equal to **half** of the circle's _____.

2. Write an expression for the base of the shape in terms of the circle's radius, *r*. Use your answer to number 1 to help. _____

3. The height of the shape is equal to the circle's _____.

4. Write your answer to number 3 as a variable. _____

You can find the area of a parallelogram by multiplying the base and the height. Try it! Find the approximate area of the shape in terms of the circle's measures.

Area ≈ base · height

Start with the formula for the area of a parallelogram.

Area ≈ _____ · _____

Substitute your answers to numbers 2 and 4 above for the base and height.

Area ≈ _____

Then simplify.

If the shape were made up of even smaller pieces, the approximate area would be even closer to the actual area of the circle!

Find the area of each triangle.

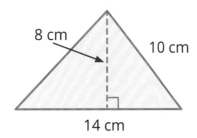

8 cm

10 cm

14 cm

A = _____

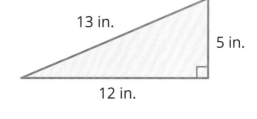

13 in.

5 in.

12 in.

A = _____

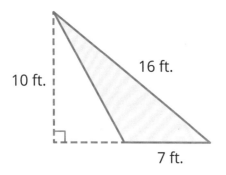

10 ft.

16 ft.

7 ft.

A = _____

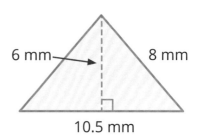

6 mm

8 mm

10.5 mm

A = _____

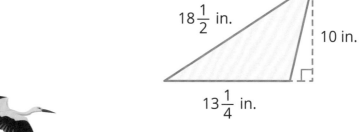

$18\frac{1}{2}$ in.

10 in.

$13\frac{1}{4}$ in.

A = _____

Find the area of each quadrilateral.

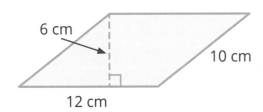

6 cm

10 cm

12 cm

$A =$ _____

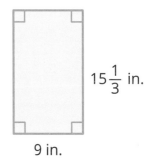

$15\frac{1}{3}$ in.

9 in.

$A =$ _____

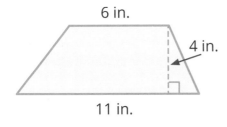

6 in.

4 in.

11 in.

$A =$ _____

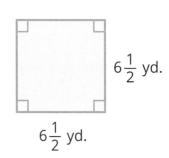

$6\frac{1}{2}$ yd.

$6\frac{1}{2}$ yd.

$A =$ _____

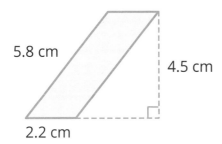

5.8 cm

4.5 cm

2.2 cm

$A =$ _____

Find the area and perimeter of each semicircle. If necessary, round your answer to the nearest hundredth.

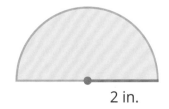

2 in.

$A \approx$ _____

$P \approx$ _____

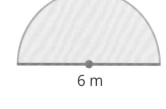

6 m

$A \approx$ _____

$P \approx$ _____

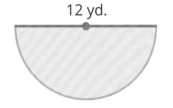

12 yd.

$A \approx$ _____

$P \approx$ _____

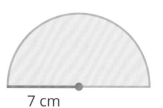

7 cm

$A \approx$ _____

$P \approx$ _____

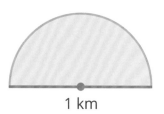

1 km

$A \approx$ _____

$P \approx$ _____

IXL.com
skill ID
SMW

Find the area of the shaded region. Use 3.14 for π.

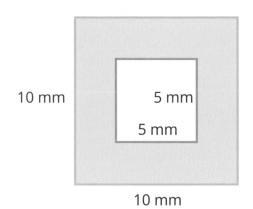

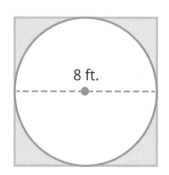

Shaded area = _____

Shaded area ≈ _____

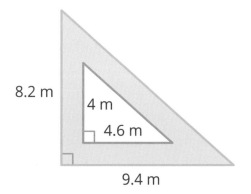

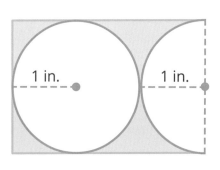

Shaded area = _____

Shaded area ≈ _____

Find the perimeter of each compound figure. Use 3.14 for π.

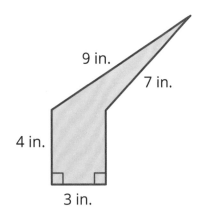

9 in.

7 in.

4 in.

3 in.

P = _____

12 mi.

12 mi.

P ≈ _____

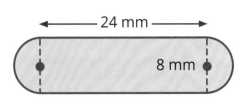

24 mm

8 mm

P ≈ _____

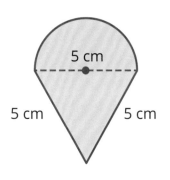

5 cm

5 cm   5 cm

P ≈ _____

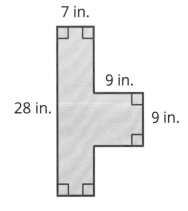

7 in.

9 in.

28 in.

9 in.

P = _____

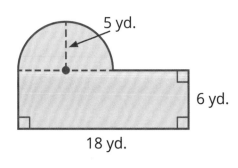

5 yd.

6 yd.

18 yd.

P ≈ _____

Keep going! Find the perimeter. Use 3.14 for π.

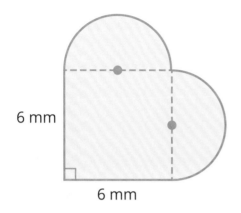

6 mm

6 mm

$P \approx$ _____

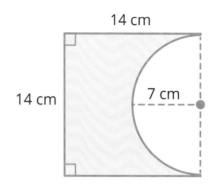

14 cm

14 cm

7 cm

$P \approx$ _____

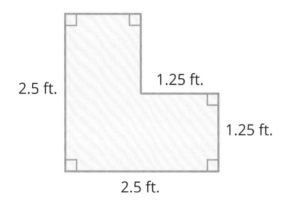

2.5 ft.

1.25 ft.

1.25 ft.

2.5 ft.

$P =$ _____

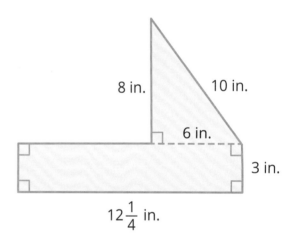

8 in.

10 in.

6 in.

3 in.

$12\frac{1}{4}$ in.

$P =$ _____

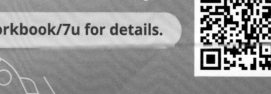

Find the area of each compound figure. Use 3.14 for π.

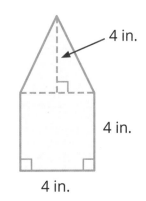

A = _____

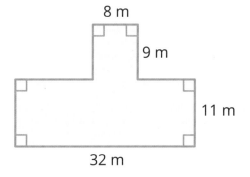

A = _____

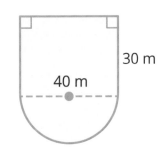

A ≈ _____

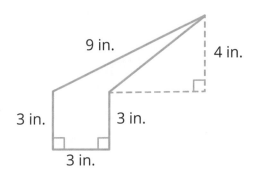

A = _____

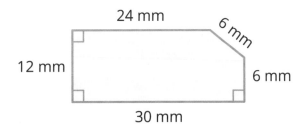

A = _____

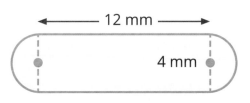

A ≈ _____

Keep going! Find the area. Use 3.14 for π.

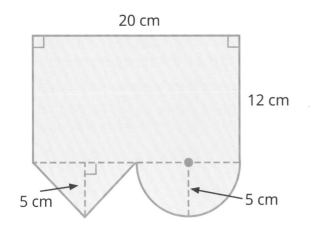

A ≈ _____

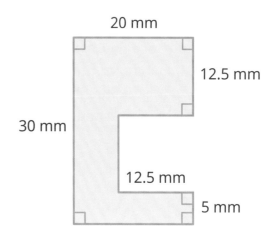

A = _____

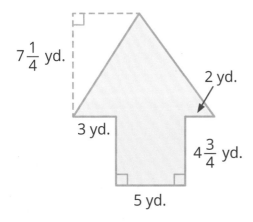

A = _____

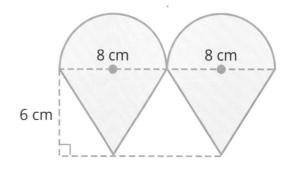

A ≈ _____

Learn!

A **scaled copy** of a figure has the same shape as the original but is a different size. The angle measures in the scaled copy are the same as the corresponding angle measures in the original figure. The side lengths of the scaled copy can be found by multiplying the corresponding side lengths in the original figure by the same number, called the **scale factor**.

Try it! Find the scale factor.

Quadrilateral *B* is a scaled copy of quadrilateral *A*.

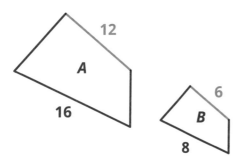

To find the scale factor, *s*, identify a pair of corresponding sides. Here, 12 and 6 are corresponding sides.

$$12s = 6$$

$$\frac{12s}{12} = \frac{6}{12}$$

$$s = \frac{1}{2}$$

Since 12 times the scale factor is equal to 6, you can use this to write and solve an equation for *s*.

So, the scale factor is $\frac{1}{2}$.

Find each scale factor.

Triangle *Z* is a scaled copy of triangle *W*.

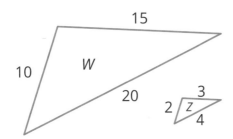

Scale factor = _____

Quadrilateral *N* is a scaled copy of quadrilateral *M*.

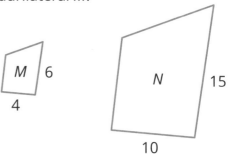

Scale factor = _____

Learn!

You can use the scale factor to find an unknown length in a scaled copy. Look at the example below.

Figure *D* is a scaled copy of figure *C*.

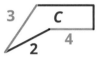
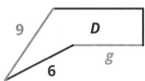

To find the unknown length, *g*, first find the scale factor, *s*.

$$3s = 9$$
$$\frac{3s}{3} = \frac{9}{3}$$
$$s = 3$$

Then multiply the corresponding side by the scale factor to find the unknown length.

$$4 \cdot 3 = g$$
$$12 = g$$

So, the value of *g* is 12.

Find each unknown length.

Pentagon *Q* is a scaled copy of pentagon *V*.

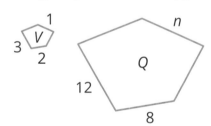

n = _____

Quadrilateral *G* is a scaled copy of quadrilateral *H*.

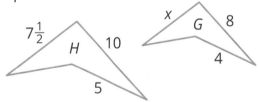

x = _____

Triangle *L* is a scaled copy of triangle *K*.

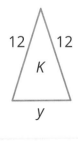
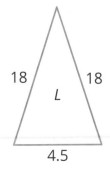

y = _____

IXL.com
skill ID
WEA

Create a scaled copy of each figure in the empty space on the grid.

Create a scaled copy of rectangle *ABCD* using a scale factor of 3.

Create a scaled copy of trapezoid *QRST* using a scale factor of 2.

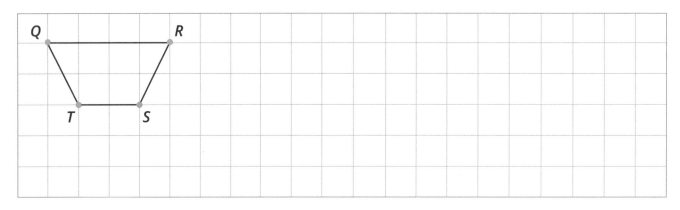

Create a scaled copy of figure *MNOP* using a scale factor of $\frac{1}{2}$.

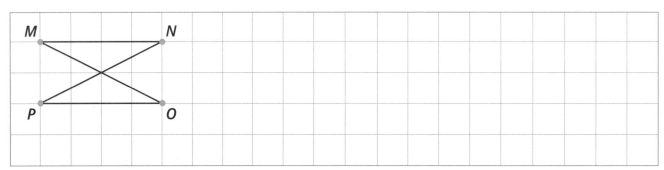

Keep going! Create a scaled copy of each figure.

Create a scaled copy of trapezoid *HIJK* using a scale factor of $\frac{1}{4}$.

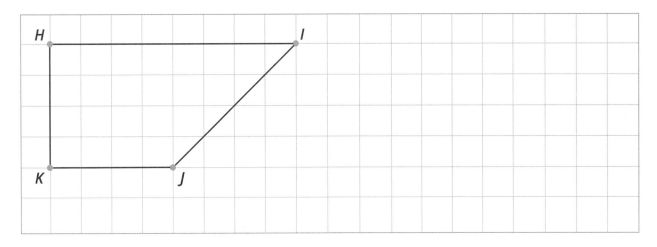

Create a scaled copy of triangle *XYZ* using a scale factor of $\frac{5}{4}$.

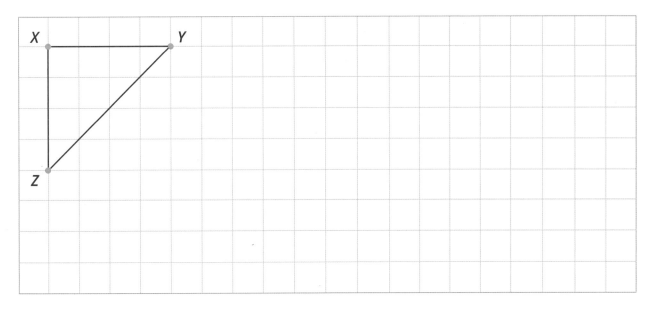

A **scale drawing** is a proportional drawing of an object. The **scale** is a ratio that compares the measurements in the drawing to the object's actual measurements. A scale can be written with a colon or equal sign, and the first quantity is usually 1 unit.

Answer each question.

On a map, the distance between Reggie's house and his school is 5 inches. The actual distance is 15 kilometers. What is the scale of the map?

$$\frac{5 \text{ in.} \div 5}{15 \text{ km} \div 5} = \frac{1 \text{ in.}}{3 \text{ km}}$$

<u>1 inch : 3 kilometers</u>

Coach Johnson made a scale drawing of Grandview Middle School's basketball court using a scale of 1 inch : 6 feet. If the width of the court is 7 inches in the drawing, what is the width of the actual court?

_____

Mateo has a poster of his favorite race car. In the poster, the length of the race car is 11 inches. The actual length of the race car is 5.5 meters. What is the scale of the poster?

_____

Pamela drew an illustration of a mountain with a scale of 1 inch : 250 meters. The actual height of the mountain is 1,500 meters. How tall is the mountain in the drawing?

_____

Kylie printed a photo of her dog, Teddy, at a scale of 3 centimeters : 2 feet. If Teddy's actual height is 3 feet, how tall is Teddy in the photo?

_____

IXL.com
skill ID
84H

You can use a scale drawing to determine the actual area of an object. First, use the scale to find the actual length and width. Then, calculate the area.

Answer each question.

What is the actual area of the checkerboard?

_____

5 cm

5 cm

Scale: 1 cm : 3 in.

What is the actual area of the tortilla chip?

_____

2.5 mm

2 mm

Scale: 1 mm : 4 cm

A bedroom measures 3 inches by 3.5 inches on a blueprint with a scale of 1 inch : 4 feet. What is the actual area of the bedroom?

_____

Ruby is painting a triangle logo on the wall of Angle Cafe. She made a drawing of the logo with a scale of 1 centimeter : $\frac{1}{2}$ of a foot. If the triangle in Ruby's drawing has a base of 10 centimeters and a height of 8 centimeters, what is the actual area of the triangle Ruby is painting?

_____

In a driver's handbook, there is a photo of a square road sign with a scale of 2 millimeters : 3 inches. In the photo, the sign measures 20 millimeters on all sides. What is the actual area of the road sign?

_____

Learn!

A **net** is a two-dimensional pattern that can be folded to create a three-dimensional figure. Look at the example. This net can be folded to make a square pyramid.

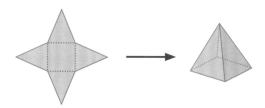

Draw a line matching the net to its 3D figure.

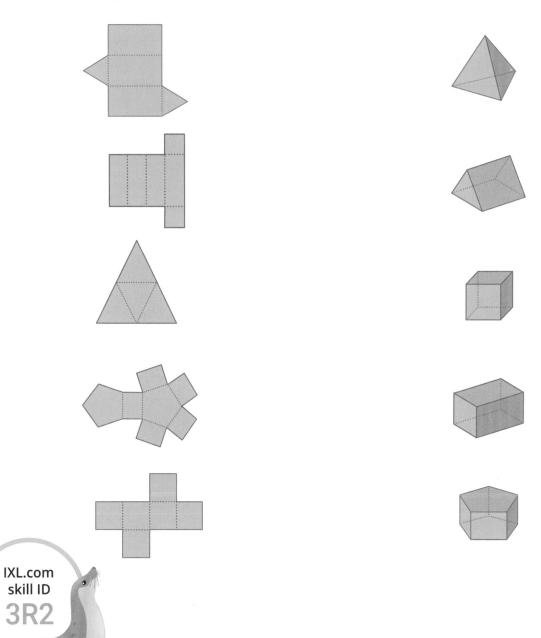

Surface area is the sum of the areas of all the faces, or surfaces, of a three-dimensional object. To find the surface area of a prism, find the area of each face. Then add the areas of all the faces. Try it! Find the surface area of the rectangular prism below.

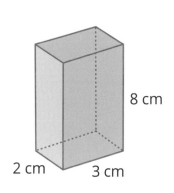

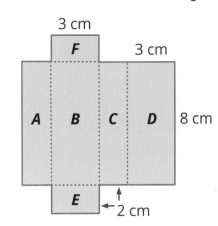

A: $2 \cdot 8 = 16$ cm²

B: $3 \cdot 8 = 24$ cm²

C: $2 \cdot 8 = 16$ cm²

D: $3 \cdot 8 = 24$ cm²

E: $3 \cdot 2 = 6$ cm²

F: $3 \cdot 2 = 6$ cm²

Surface area = 16 + 24 + 16 + 24 + 6 + 6 = 92 cm²

So, the surface area of the rectangular prism is 92 square centimeters.

Find the surface area of each prism.

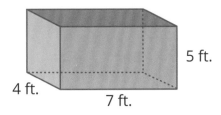

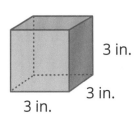

Surface area = _____

Surface area = _____

Keep going! Find the surface area of each prism.

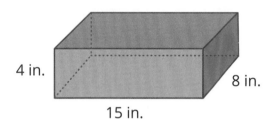

4 in.
8 in.
15 in.

Surface area = _____

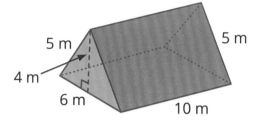

5 m
5 m
4 m
6 m
10 m

Surface area = _____

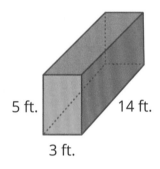

5 ft.
14 ft.
3 ft.

Surface area = _____

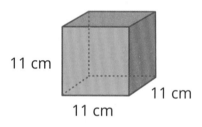

11 cm
11 cm
11 cm

Surface area = _____

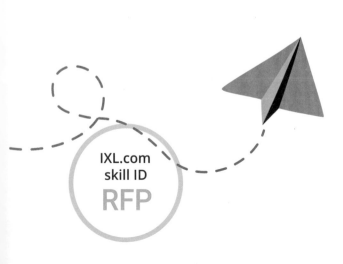

15 yd.
12 yd.
20 yd.
9 yd.

Surface area = _____

Keep going! Find the surface area of each prism.

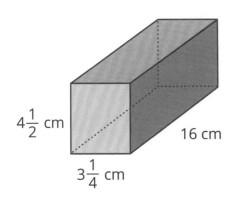

$4\frac{1}{2}$ cm

$3\frac{1}{4}$ cm

16 cm

Surface area = _____

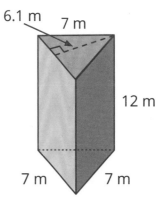

6.1 m   7 m

12 m

7 m   7 m

Surface area = _____

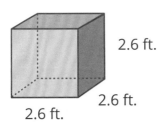

2.6 ft.

2.6 ft.

2.6 ft.

Surface area = _____

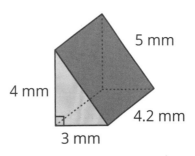

5 mm

4 mm

4.2 mm

3 mm

Surface area = _____

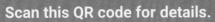

Learn!

You can find the surface area of a pyramid, too. Find the area of each face. Then add the areas of all the faces together. Try it! Find the surface area of the triangular pyramid below.

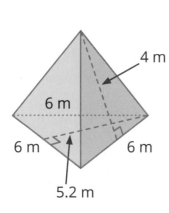

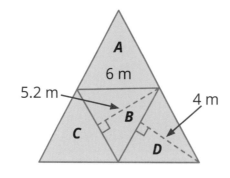

A: $\frac{1}{2} \cdot 6 \cdot 4 = 12$ m²

B: $\frac{1}{2} \cdot 6 \cdot 5.2 = 15.6$ m²

C: $\frac{1}{2} \cdot 6 \cdot 4 = 12$ m²

D: $\frac{1}{2} \cdot 6 \cdot 4 = 12$ m²

Surface area = 12 + 15.6 + 12 + 12 = 51.6 m²

So, the surface area of the triangular pyramid is 51.6 square meters.

Find the surface area of each pyramid.

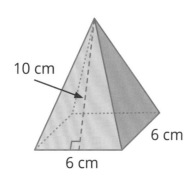

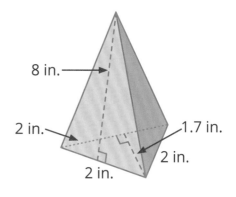

Surface area = _____

Surface area = _____

Keep going! Find the surface area of each pyramid.

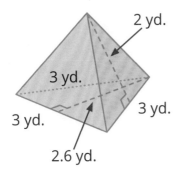

Surface area = _____

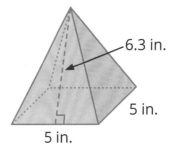

Surface area = _____

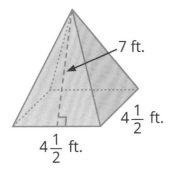

Surface area = _____

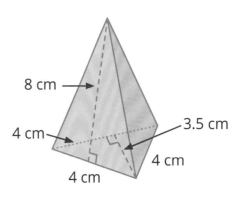

Surface area = _____

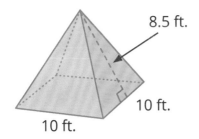

Surface area = _____

IXL.com
skill ID
XSJ

Calculate the surface area of each three-dimensional figure.

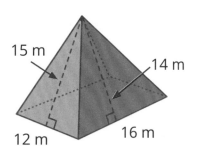

15 m

14 m

12 m

16 m

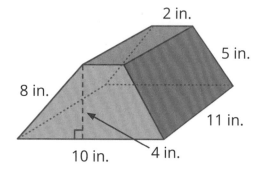

2 in.

5 in.

8 in.

11 in.

10 in.

4 in.

Surface area = _____

Surface area = _____

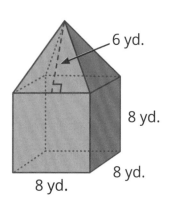

6 yd.

8 yd.

8 yd.

8 yd.

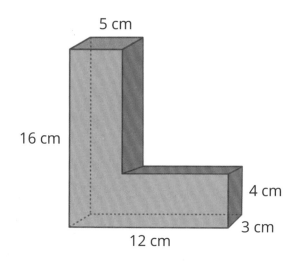

5 cm

16 cm

4 cm

3 cm

12 cm

Surface area = _____

Surface area = _____

Answer each question.

Malia is painting a wooden pyramid for an art project. The pyramid has a square base with side lengths of 5 feet, and each triangle has a height of 4 feet. What is the total area that Malia will need to paint?

_____

Rebecca bought _Dino Legend_ to give to her sister for her birthday. The game comes in a case that is in the shape of a rectangular prism. It measures 7 inches long, 5 inches wide, and $\frac{1}{2}$ of an inch deep. How much wrapping paper does Rebecca need to cover the case without any gaps or overlaps?

_____

Tent Factory makes camping tents shaped like triangular prisms. Their most popular tent has a rectangular floor measuring 6 feet by 8 feet, two rectangular walls measuring 5 feet by 8 feet, and two triangular panels with a height of 4 feet. What is the total area of material needed for all the sections of this tent?

_____

Emily built a wooden jewelry box in the shape of a cube. Each side of the box measures 12.5 centimeters. Emily stained the outside of the box, including the lid, but she did not stain the bottom of the box. What is the area that Emily stained?

_____

Learn!

Volume is the amount of space an object takes up. It is measured in cubic units. To find the volume of a prism, multiply the area of the base, *B*, by the height of the prism, *h*. You can use the formula **V = Bh**. Try it! Find the volume of the triangular prism.

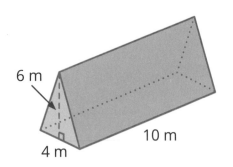

The base of the prism is a triangle with a height of 6 meters and a base of 4 meters. Find the area of the base, *B*.

$$B = \frac{1}{2} \cdot 4 \cdot 6 = 12 \text{ m}^2$$

The height of the prism, *h*, is the distance between its two bases, which is 10 meters.

$$V = 12 \cdot 10 = 120 \text{ m}^3$$

So, the volume of the triangular prism is 120 cubic meters.

Find the volume of each prism.

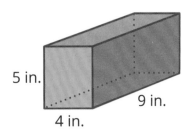

5 in.

9 in.

4 in.

V = _____

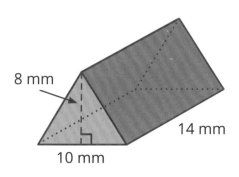

8 mm

14 mm

10 mm

V = _____

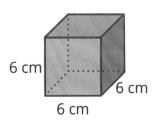

6 cm

6 cm

6 cm

V = _____

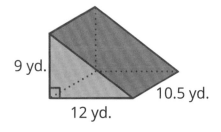

9 yd.

10.5 yd.

12 yd.

V = _____

Find the volume of each prism.

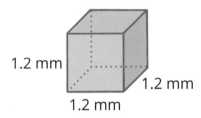

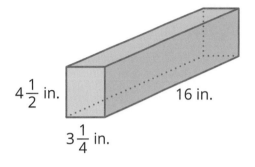

V = _____

V = _____

Use the volume to find the missing dimension of each prism.

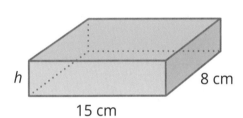

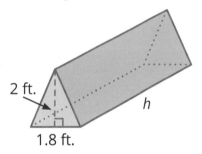

V = 360 cm³

V = 9 ft.³

h = _____

h = _____

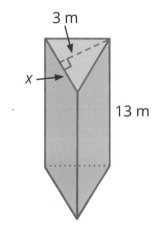

V = 78 m³

x = _____

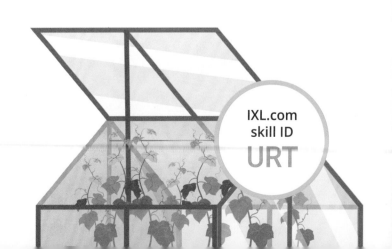

Learn!

To find the volume of a pyramid, multiply $\frac{1}{3}$ by the area of the base, B, and the height of the pyramid, h. You can use the formula $V = \frac{1}{3}Bh$. Try it! Find the volume of the rectangular pyramid below.

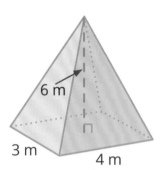

The base of the pyramid is a rectangle with a length of 4 meters and a width of 3 meters. Find the area of the base, B.

$$B = 3 \cdot 4 = 12 \text{ m}^2$$

The height of the pyramid, h, is 6 meters.

$$V = \frac{1}{3} \cdot 12 \cdot 6 = 24 \text{ m}^3$$

So, the volume of the rectangular pyramid is 24 cubic meters.

Find the volume of each pyramid.

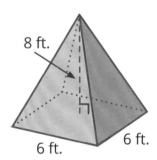

$V =$ _____

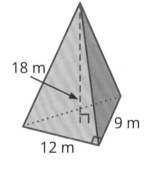

$V =$ _____

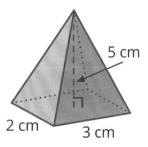

$V =$ _____

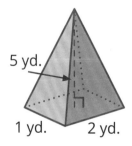

$V =$ _____

Keep going! Find the volume of each pyramid.

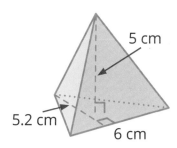

$V =$ _____

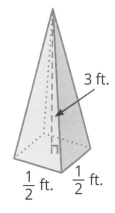

$V =$ _____

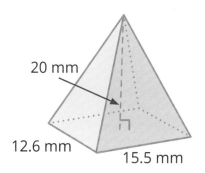

$V =$ _____

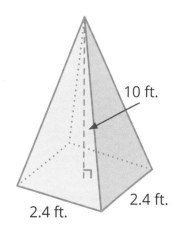

$V =$ _____

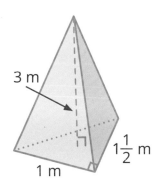

$V =$ _____

Find the volume of each figure.

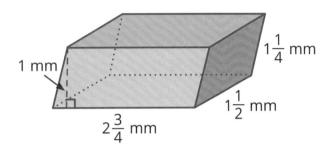

$1\frac{1}{4}$ mm

1 mm

$1\frac{1}{2}$ mm

$2\frac{3}{4}$ mm

V = _____

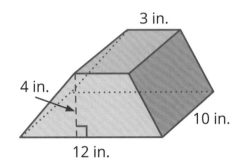

3 in.

4 in.

10 in.

12 in.

V = _____

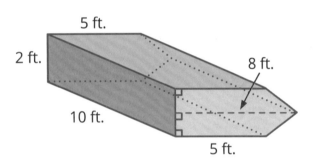

5 ft.

2 ft.

8 ft.

10 ft.

5 ft.

V = _____

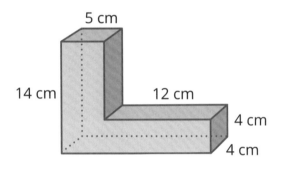

5 cm

14 cm

12 cm

4 cm

4 cm

V = _____

IXL.com
skill ID
EP5

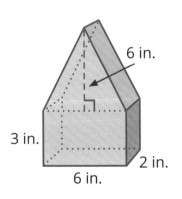

6 in.

3 in.

6 in.

2 in.

V = _____

Answer each question.

Quincy is moving and needs to pack up everything in his bedroom. He was able to fit all of his games into one box that measures 15 inches along each edge. What is the volume of the box?

_____

Jenn is curious about the volume of one of her tents, which is shaped like a rectangular pyramid. The base measures 3 meters by 4 meters, and the tent is 2 meters tall. What is the volume of the tent?

_____

Sadie is choosing between two storage containers to help her organize her closet. She can use a storage container shaped like a rectangular prism measuring 1.5 feet tall, 2.7 feet wide, and 6 feet long, or she can use a storage container shaped like a cube measuring 3 feet along each side. Which container has more storage space?

_____

The square pyramid sculpture at the Raymond City Museum has a volume of 40 cubic yards. The square base measures 5 yards on each side. How tall is the pyramid sculpture?

_____

IXL.com
skill ID
8WV

A **cross section** is a two-dimensional shape that is formed when a three-dimensional figure is sliced. Determine the shape of each cross section.

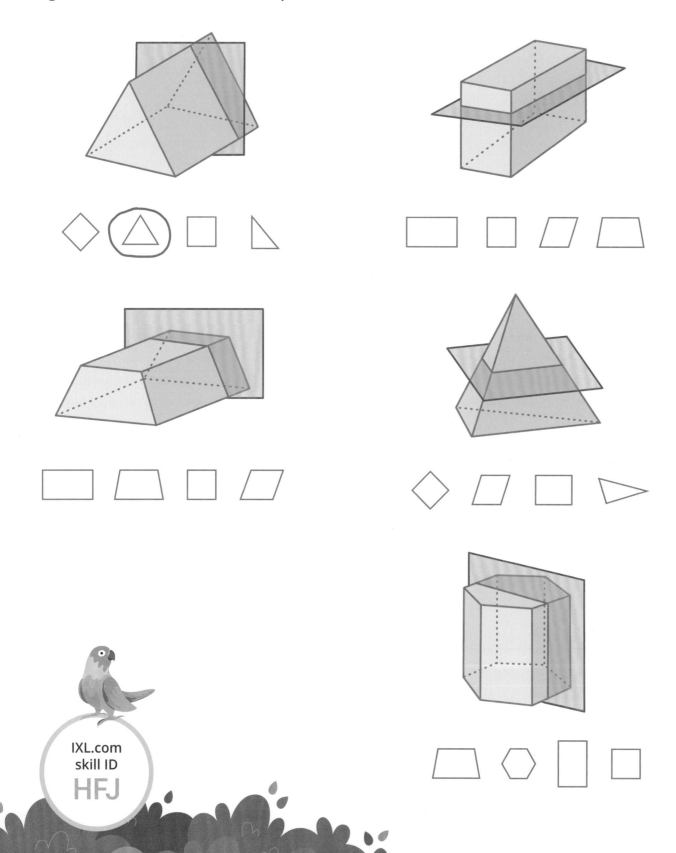

Draw the shape of each cross section.

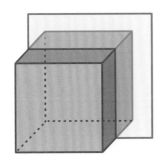 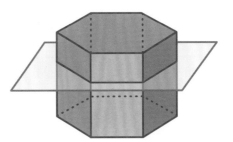

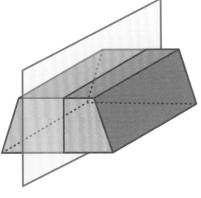 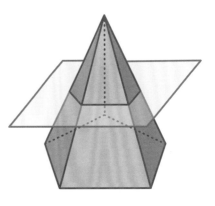

Time for review! Add, subtract, multiply, or divide.

5.2 + 7.1 = _____

−28 ÷ 2 = _____

−6 × (−7) = _____

$-\dfrac{1}{3} \times \dfrac{2}{9} =$ _____

$\dfrac{5}{6} + \left(-\dfrac{7}{12}\right) =$ _____

$-\dfrac{1}{10} \div \dfrac{5}{6} =$ _____

$-\dfrac{2}{7} \times \left(-\dfrac{7}{10}\right) =$ _____

6 − (−34) = _____

1.82 ÷ (−1.3) = _____

$2\dfrac{2}{5} \times \left(-3\dfrac{2}{3}\right) =$ _____

$-\dfrac{3}{10} \div \left(-\dfrac{11}{20}\right) =$ _____

$-14\dfrac{1}{8} - 11\dfrac{3}{4} =$ _____

$-10\dfrac{2}{5} - (-17.2) =$ _____

$-1.2 \times \left(-8\dfrac{1}{4}\right) =$ _____

$-4.9 + \dfrac{5}{8} =$ _____

Solve each set of problems. Then write your answers in the puzzle below. Your answers will share a digit. Each digit, decimal point, and negative sign goes in its own box.

19.25 − (−3.78) = ___23.03___   57 + (−6.02) = _____

−15.16 + 11.26 = ___−3.9___   −9.4 × (−5.3) = _____

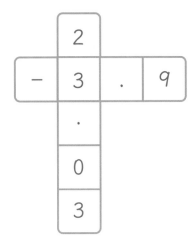
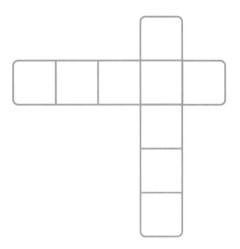

−18.6 ÷ 4 = _____   −8.1 × (−2.9) = _____

−83 ÷ (−12.5) = _____   −16.7 − 17.4 = _____

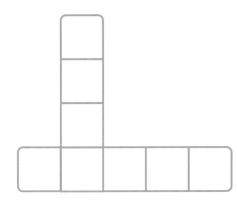
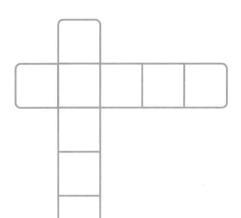

IXL.com
skill ID
5ZF

Solving equations

Solve each equation.

$5x + 12 = 27$

$11a - 15 = 84$

$\frac{h}{5} + 9 = 8$

$1 = -7k + 8$

$-13m - 4 = 35$

$3(p + 6) = 36$

$5n - 5.3 = -2.8$

$-\frac{1}{3} = -2b - \frac{5}{6}$

$12(c - 9) = -60$

$-1.5(v + 10) = 15$

$4z - \frac{1}{2} = 1$

$-(4r - 91) = 27$

IXL.com skill ID **66R**

Luna and her family spent the day at Fun World Theme Park. Write and solve an equation for each problem.

Luna's mom bought tickets for all 4 family members. After she used a coupon for $20 off the entire purchase, the total cost was $80. What was the original price, *t*, of each ticket?

_____

First, Luna went on the Ferris wheel. She spent a total of 11 minutes on the ride, including the 5 minutes that it took to board and unload passengers. If each revolution took 1.5 minutes, how many revolutions, *r*, did the Ferris wheel make?

_____

For lunch, Luna's family decided to eat at Pizza Town. The total cost of their meal was $24.25. They left the waiter a 20% tip. How much money, *m*, did they spend on lunch, including tip?

_____

Before heading home, Luna, her brother, and her sister each picked out a key chain to remember their day. Each key chain cost *k* dollars, but Luna's mom had a coupon for 30% off the total cost. If she paid a total of $15.75, what was the original cost of each key chain?

_____

Luna's favorite part of the day was playing games at Fun World Theme Park. Read about the games Luna played. Then answer each question.

In the first game Luna played, she threw 3 rings, and all 3 landed on the same stake! So, she got to spin the prize wheel. The wheel featured 20 equal-sized sections. There were 13 sections with no prize, 6 sections with small prizes, and 1 section with a large prize.

Luna landed on a section that won a prize. What was the probability of that happening?

_____

Luna won a large prize! What was the probability of that happening?

_____

In the second game Luna played, she threw a ball at a target. If she hit the center, 1 random ball would be released out of a cage and down a chute. The color of the ball determined which prize Luna won. The table shows the color of the ball that dropped down the chute for each player who played before Luna.

Color	Yellow	Green	White	Orange	Red
Frequency	10	3	1	7	4

Based on this data, if 200 players play the game, how many times would you expect a white ball to drop down the chute?

_____

Based on this data, if 50 balls are in the cage, how many would you expect to be green?

_____

Luna got an orange ball. Based on this data, what was the probability of that happening?

_____

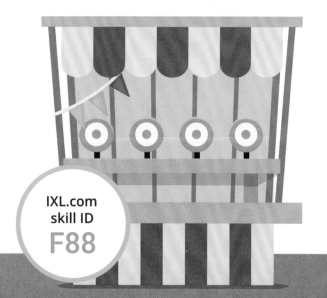

Keep going! Answer each question.

In the third game Luna played, she flipped a coin onto a game board. The game board had 5 equal sections numbered 1 to 5. Prizes were awarded based on how the coin landed (heads or tails) and the section of the game board the coin landed on.

Use a tree diagram, table, or organized list to find the sample space.

There are _____ possible outcomes in the sample space.

According to the rules of the game, players do not win a prize if they land on heads in an odd-numbered section. What is the probability of that happening?   _____

Players win the grand prize if they land on tails in section 3 or 5. What is the probability of that happening?   _____

Luna landed on tails in section 4. What was the probability of that happening?

_____

Determine the constant of proportionality, *k*, for each proportional relationship.

x	1	2	3	5
y	2	4	6	10

k = _____

$y = 7x$

k = _____

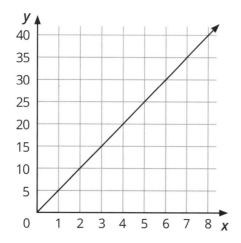

k = _____

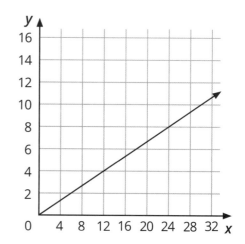

k = _____

$y = \dfrac{3}{5}x$

k = _____

x	5	10	25	50
y	2.95	5.9	14.75	29.5

k = _____

Benny is excited to play a new video game called *Detective Dash*. In this game, Benny plays a detective who must solve mysteries, collect coins, and earn points.

Read the descriptions below and determine whether each relationship is proportional.

The detective begins the game with 3 items in a briefcase: a notepad, a magnifying glass, and a camera. As mysteries are solved, more items are collected. The graph shows the number of mysteries solved, x, and the number of items in the detective's briefcase, y.

Is the relationship proportional?

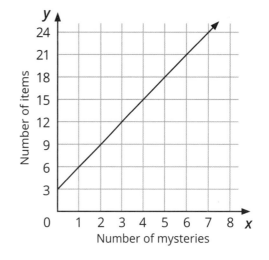

Benny earns points in the game for every mystery he solves. The equation shows the relationship between the number of mysteries Benny solves, x, and the number of points he earns, y.

Is the relationship proportional?

$$y = 10x$$

Additional clues can be purchased to help solve a mystery. The table shows the relationship between the number of clues Benny purchased, x, and the number of coins he spent, y.

x	2	3	5	6
y	16	24	40	48

Is the relationship proportional?

Benny must search for clues in order to solve every mystery in *Detective Dash*. He earns 3 coins for every clue he finds. The relationship between the number of clues Benny finds, x, and the number of coins earned, y, is proportional.

Complete the table. Then graph the relationship on the coordinate plane.

Number of clues	Number of coins
2	
4	
8	
16	

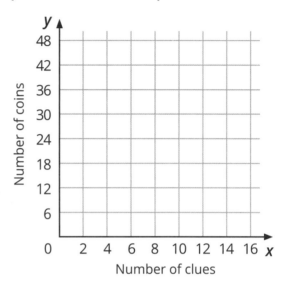

Answer each question.

Write an equation with x and y to describe the relationship. _____

Write the ordered pair of the point on the line with an x-coordinate of 1.   (_____ , _____)

This point means when Benny finds _____ clue, he earns _____ coins.

Write the ordered pair of the point on the line with a y-coordinate of 36.   (_____ , _____)

This point means when Benny finds _____ clues, he earns _____ coins.

Benny loves playing *Detective Dash*, so he decides to buy some merchandise. He spends $12 on 8 of his favorite stickers. The relationship between the number of stickers Benny purchases, *x*, and the total cost, *y*, is proportional.

Complete the table. Then graph the relationship on the coordinate plane.

Number of stickers	Cost ($)
2	
4	
6	
8	

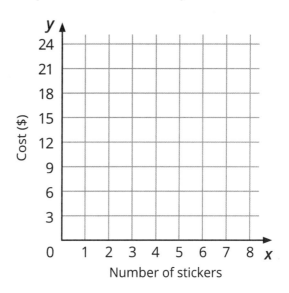

Answer each question.

Write an equation with *x* and *y* to describe the relationship. _____

How much does each sticker cost? _____

Write this as an ordered pair. (_____ , _____)

How much money would Benny pay for 3 stickers? _____

Write this as an ordered pair. (_____ , _____)

Answer key

Rational numbers can be written in different ways. This answer key includes fractions and mixed numbers that are in simplest form. Keep in mind that there may be other equivalent answers that are also correct.

PAGE 4

integer	rational
rational	integer
rational	rational
whole	whole
rational	rational
whole	integer

PAGE 5

True
False
True
True
False
True
True
False
True
False
True
True
True

PAGE 6

0.6	$-0.\overline{2}$	0.875

PAGE 7

0.75	$-0.5\overline{6}$	$0.7\overline{3}$
$0.\overline{36}$	2.625	0.675
$5.41\overline{6}$	$-3.2\overline{7}$	-7.4

PAGE 8

-8		35	-42
$-1\frac{1}{8}$		$\frac{3}{10}$	0.1

26	73	22	30
$-\frac{2}{15}$	7.1	-1.9	$3\frac{2}{5}$

$|-26|$	Opposite of 2
$\left|-\frac{7}{8}\right|$	$|-2.97|$
	Opposite of 11.8

PAGE 9

Not zero
Zero
Zero
Not zero
Not zero

Answers will vary. One possible answer is shown below.

Tony has $4\frac{1}{2}$ cups of flour in his pantry. He uses $4\frac{1}{2}$ cups of flour to make a loaf of bread. How much flour does he have left?

PAGE 10

$6 + (-1) = 5$

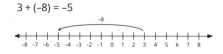

$-2 + 6 = 4$

$-8 + 5 = -3$

$-2 + (-4) = -6$

$3 + (-8) = -5$

PAGE 11

-59	-10	65
-55	27	-10
-12	-30	-71
13	-89	-4
54	-5	36

PAGE 12

$6 - (-1) = 7$

$-5 - 1 = -6$

PAGE 12, *continued*

$-2 - (-7) = 5$

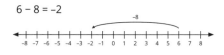

$6 - 8 = -2$

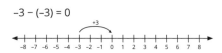

$-3 - (-3) = 0$

PAGE 13

-2	-28	-10
-22	-1	-50
-46	65	-27
75	-39	87
30	80	-67

PAGE 14

-5	11	7
-16	-12	28
-51	-24	-2
-60	18	-100
41	19	24
-77	-76	-22
-14	-131	13
-16	-64	-36

PAGE 15

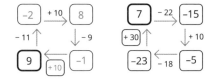

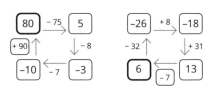

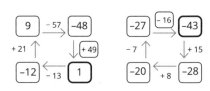

PAGE 16

2.6	–12.5	1.7
–3.7	–12.1	0.1
4.5	–2.7	–12
–19.1	–0.9	15.07
0	4.84	–16.8
	1.175	–6.024

PAGE 17

$-\frac{3}{7}$	$-\frac{4}{5}$	$\frac{2}{9}$
$-\frac{1}{6}$	$3\frac{7}{9}$	$9\frac{1}{3}$
$-5\frac{1}{3}$	$-3\frac{1}{8}$	$2\frac{11}{16}$
$4\frac{3}{20}$	$1\frac{3}{10}$	$3\frac{1}{4}$
$6\frac{1}{15}$	$1\frac{17}{40}$	$4\frac{7}{12}$
$-5\frac{5}{16}$	$-6\frac{13}{24}$	

PAGE 18

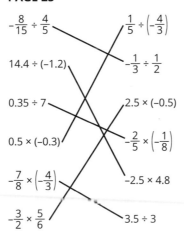

PAGE 19

Answers may vary. All answers are provided in decimal form.

7.75	–5.6
–4.7	0.25
–5.5	–0.35
–16.78	2.72
2.37	–7.54
–16.65	

PAGE 20

–15 points

–6 feet

12.7 milliliters

$27.50

79.8°F

PAGE 21

–15	40	–6
8	28	–9
–60	36	–11
–10	–160	3
–30	14	–240
–210	220	

PAGE 22

60	49	–350
6	120	–3
–96	40	400
–4	–32	–9
720	–5	–280
–70	–180	2
132	7	–135
–3	–4	–3

PAGE 23

0.62	86
–8.9	7.5
–39	–15.12
–9.72	–9.3
3.115	–24.2

PAGE 24

$-\frac{3}{40}$	$-\frac{3}{4}$
–2	$\frac{8}{21}$
$6\frac{3}{4}$	$2\frac{2}{9}$
$-\frac{3}{4}$	$\frac{1}{4}$
$-\frac{2}{9}$	$-7\frac{1}{3}$

PAGE 25

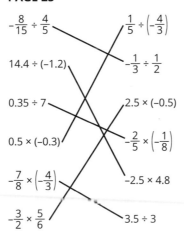

PAGE 26

Answers may vary. All answers are provided in decimal form.

1.3	–4.5
0.45	11.5
–11.1	–10.25
14.4	13.9
	–57.4

PAGE 27

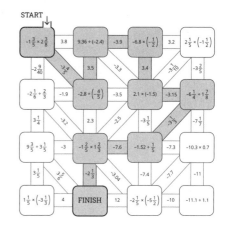

PAGE 28

–300

–185

28

$1\frac{3}{4}$

–16.2

–54.6

PAGE 29

2	–5	–18
17	–74	–43
–55	24	9
30	–42	–4
21	129	–63
2	–6	–8
–2	–40	–17
34	–141	

Answer key

PAGE 30

Explanations may vary. Some possible explanations are shown below.

Diego divided instead of multiplying.

$-2 \times 4 = -8$

Joy made a mistake when adding the opposite. She added 2 instead of adding –2.

$-5 - 2 = -5 + (-2) = -7$

PAGE 31

2.4	$-5\frac{1}{6}$	–16.1
$-\frac{1}{4}$	–6.5	–12.8
$-6\frac{1}{2}$	–9	$-14\frac{1}{8}$
–3.5	$-5\frac{5}{8}$	–54
$-\frac{1}{24}$	7.95	$-8\frac{4}{5}$
25	$2\frac{1}{12}$	–13.58

PAGE 32

Answers may vary. All answers are provided in decimal form.

–2.2	102	–0.51
–32	–7.3	5.6
–40.32	–19	0
3.04	–15.66	–14.445

PAGE 33

7.02	$-1\frac{4}{9}$
–55	–55.18
0.23	4
–2.6	

PAGE 34

8 flowers per vase

12 books per shelf

4 windows per apartment

68 miles per hour

16 pencils per pack

$1\frac{1}{2}$ lawns per hour

14 players per team

$2\frac{1}{4}$ gallons per tank

9 carrots per bag

8 chairs per table

$\frac{1}{2}$ minute per lap

6 drawers per dresser

4 socks per package

PAGE 35

$3.99 per bag

$4.85 per gallon

$0.95 per battery

$12.75 per T-shirt

$0.75 per sponge

$1.45 per pound

$2.50 per ticket

$3.40 per square foot

8 protein bars for $11.84

$1.68 for 7 paintbrushes

$32.48 for 8 boxes of dog treats

$1.44 for 16 ounces of apple juice

PAGE 36

$\frac{1}{4}$ liters per glass

$\frac{1}{12}$ cups per teaspoon

$\frac{1}{6}$ cups per gallon

2 hours per room

$2\frac{1}{4}$ sticks per batch

$1\frac{3}{4}$ miles per hour

2 pounds per pot

$\frac{3}{4}$ tubs per dozen

PAGE 37

6 miles

$20

$\frac{1}{2}$ of an onion

4 meters per second

2 cups

$3\frac{1}{5}$ feet

PAGE 38

20	24	18
16	42	16
35	2	1
9	49	5
23	7	1
5	2	$3\frac{1}{2}$
0.9	26	$9\frac{1}{5}$
39	$7\frac{2}{3}$	6

PAGE 39

(6:8 and 3:4)

(15:8 and 5:6)

(3:7 and 9:21)

(28:8 and 14:4)

3:7 and 18:35

(9:6 and 36:24)

6:15 and 12:25

(16:10 and 48:30)

32:42 and 16:22

(15:20 and 6:8)

(16:24 and 14:21)

3.5:4.5 and 8:9

$\frac{12}{5}$:3 and 13:15

(1.6:8 and 0.8:4)

PAGE 40

$q = 24$	$g = 12$	$p = 40$
$k = 8$	$m = 40$	$s = 56$

PAGE 41

$f = 6$	$d = 33$	$n = 11.2$
$b = 28.5$	$a = 22.4$	$y = 3$
$x = 3.2$	$c = 38$	$v = 6.65$

PAGE 42

No	Yes	No
Yes	No	Yes

PAGE 43

Yes	No	No
Yes	Yes	No

PAGE 44

$k = 5$	$k = 3$	$k = 6$
	$k = \frac{1}{3}$	$k = \frac{3}{2}$

PAGE 45

$k = \frac{4}{7}$	$k = 1.2$	$k = \frac{5}{6}$
$k = 4.5$	$k = \frac{3}{5}$	$k = 8$

PAGE 46

$y = 4x$	$y = 9x$	$y = \frac{2}{3}x$
	$y = 3x$	$y = \frac{3}{4}x$

PAGE 47

$y = \frac{3}{4}x$

$y = 8x$

$y = 5.15x$

$y = 6x$

$y = \frac{2}{3}x$

PAGE 48

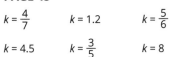

$y = \frac{2}{5}x$ 20 lemons

$y = 3x$ 30 tickets

$y = 10.50x$ $52.50

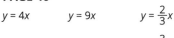

$y = \frac{9}{2}x$ 8 purses

PAGE 49

No	Yes
No	Yes

PAGE 50

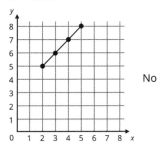

No

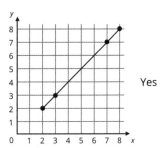

Yes

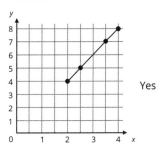

No

PAGE 51

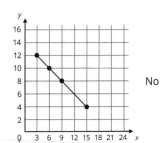

Yes

No

PAGE 51, *continued*

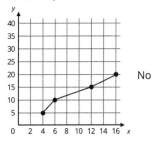

No

PAGE 52

$k = 2$	$k = 1$

PAGE 53

$k = \frac{1}{2}$	$k = \frac{1}{5}$
$k = \frac{4}{3}$	$k = \frac{5}{16}$

PAGE 54

$y = 3x$	$y = 4x$
$y = \frac{1}{15}x$	$y = \frac{4}{3}x$

PAGE 55

$y = 2x$	$y = 2.25x$
$y = \frac{1}{3}x$	

PAGE 56

A vegetable medley with 3 cups of carrots also has 6 cups of peas.

A vegetable medley with 1 cup of carrots also has 2 cups of peas.

5 shelves can hold 30 books.
0 shelves can hold 0 books.

A fish tank with 50 gallons of water can hold 30 fish.

A fish tank with 25 gallons of water can hold 15 fish.

PAGE 57

8 videos
10 minutes

3 fire trucks
6 race cars

3 weeks

$0

Answer key

PAGE 58

$y = 3x$

Number of events	Number of ribbons ordered
1	3
2	6
3	9
5	15
7	21

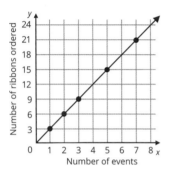

(4, 12)
This point means that 12 ribbons would be ordered for 4 events.

(6, 18)
This point means that 18 ribbons would be ordered for 6 events.

PAGE 59

$y = 4x$

Number of students	Number of orange slices
5	20
10	40
20	80
25	100
35	140

PAGE 59, *continued*

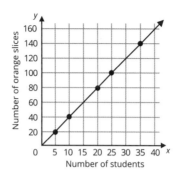

4 orange slices
(1, 4)

96 orange slices
(24, 96)

PAGE 60

Fraction	Decimal	Percent
$\frac{43}{100}$	0.43	43%
$\frac{9}{100}$	0.09	9%
$\frac{4}{5}$	0.8	80%
$\frac{7}{20}$	0.35	35%
$\frac{1}{4}$	0.25	25%
$\frac{1}{100}$	0.01	1%
$\frac{16}{25}$	0.64	64%
$\frac{13}{1,100}$	0.013	1.3%
$\frac{11}{10}$ or $1\frac{1}{10}$	1.1	110%
$\frac{7}{4}$ or $1\frac{3}{4}$	1.75	175%
$\frac{1}{8}$	0.125	12.5%

PAGE 61

6	18	12
13	12	21
4.4	11	90
33	0.7	

PAGE 62

20	45
24	5
25.2	400
	4

PAGE 63

$0.63
$3.60
$1.98
$20.90

PAGE 64

25% decrease
20% increase
60% decrease
12.5% decrease
150% increase

PAGE 65

$80
40 points
31.25 hours

PAGE 66

30% off any instrument
$40 off any printer
10% off any tent
$30 off new memberships
$5 off any meal

PAGE 67

$62.30
80%
64%
$1.83
$63

PAGE 68

75%
40%
4%
20%
25%

215

PAGE 69

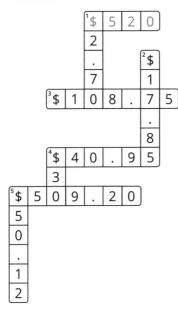

PAGE 70

$3,150

$5,900

$952.50

$342

PAGE 71

	Starting amount	Interest	Balance
Year 1	$1,000	$100	$1,100
Year 2	$1,100	$110	$1,210
Year 3	$1,210	$121	$1,331
Year 4	$1,331	$133.10	$1,464.10
Year 5	$1,464.10	$146.41	$1,610.51

$610.51

$500

Answers will vary. One possible answer is shown below.

One situation when you might want to have compound interest is when you are saving money. A situation where you might not want to have compound interest is if you are borrowing money.

PAGE 72

3   −10

a and d −3

−7 c and t

PAGE 72, *continued*

−5.8   3 terms

3 terms   1

23.1 $-6\frac{4}{7}$

                     j and w

                     $-\frac{1}{4}$

                     4 terms

PAGE 73

32   −4

−1 $3\frac{1}{4}$

$13\frac{1}{8}$ 0

−13

22

−0.7

PAGE 74

−8x − 24   4t − 20

6m + 6   −6v + 12

−32 + 12q 24f + 36

−2 − 2n 56b − 42

4c − 4   42g − 36

                     45 − 81a

PAGE 75

80 − 48p −3c − 13

−3a − 2   12h − 4

−8 + 12p −4.2t + 2.4

1.1n + 3.3j −11 −21b + 15z − 3

−2s + 5 + q −21 − 17j − 5m

PAGE 76

6(x + 3)   7(2y + 1)   5(q − 16)

13(2t − 1)   4(4 − n)   10(7 − 6k)

24(2 − 3w)   9(9g + 5)   6(4p − 9)

PAGE 77

2(2c − 3s + 4)   3(2q + 4w + m)

8(6r − 2 − 5d)   11(4 − 9b − 3t)

9(9k − g + 3h)   7(6 − 7a − 12x)

4(2 + 4w − 3v)   6(5u − 3t − 7)

2(13n + 17y − p)

PAGE 78

11x − 12   5p

16g − 6   4c + 2k

4   30t + 30

9 + 3m 3v − d + 1

6t − 5y + 2   −4k + 3j

−r + 5   6.4g − 3h

PAGE 79

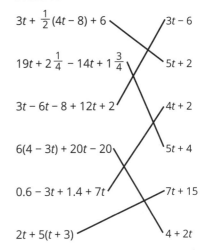

PAGE 80

6x + 2   6y + 3

5 + 2h 10.3 + 16.2p

10n − 2j $\frac{1}{2}a$ + 8z

11f + 2v + 3.4

PAGE 81

3c + 8   8 − 8a

3s − 1.6 $\frac{1}{8}t$ + 9

−5 − 6v + 1.2w

PAGE 82

b(1 + 0.3) b + 30

b + 0.3b 1.3b

2m + 20   2m + 40 − 20

2(m + 40) − 20 m + 40 + m − 20

0.85p 0.15p

p(1 + 0.15) p − 0.15p

30d 3(d + 10)

3d + 30   3 + d + 10

PAGE 82, *continued*

Expressions may vary. Some possible expressions are shown below.

$b + \frac{30}{100}b$

$m + m + 20$

$p(1 - 0.15)$

$3d + 3(10)$

PAGE 83

Expressions may vary. Some possible expressions are shown below.

$t + 0.05t$	336 tickets
$1.05t$	

$c - 0.2c$	$372.64
$0.8c$	

$g + \frac{1}{2}g + 12$	18 students
$\frac{3}{2}g + 12$	

PAGE 84

$t = 7$	$w = 10$	$q = -10$
$x = -3$	$p = 2$	$m = -6$
$s = 6$	$z = 11.9$	$n = 11.5$
$d = \frac{3}{10}$	$b = \frac{11}{12}$	$v = 1.4$
$f = -\frac{7}{4}$	$y = -2\frac{1}{4}$	$h = 6.44$

PAGE 85

$s = 3$	$m = 32$	$a = -2$
$f = -24$	$k = 11$	$p = -15$
$g = 0.7$	$n = 72$	$x = -23$
$c = 32$	$y = -21.6$	$j = 75$
$t = \frac{2}{3}$	$r = -3.3$	$v = \frac{1}{12}$

PAGE 86

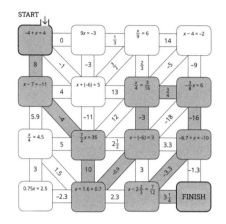

PAGE 87

Equations may vary. Some possible equations are shown below.

$2.7 + p = 18$

15.3 pounds

$m - 12 = 4$

16 miles

$-3h = -18$

6 hours

$n - 12 = -39$

−27 meters

$\frac{2}{5}j = 14$

35 jelly beans

PAGE 88

$y = 3$	$f = 4$	$w = 11$
$h = 2$	$b = -4$	$k = 5$
$d = 7$	$m = -6$	$t = -8$

PAGE 89

$c = 27$	$v = 6.8$	$u = -96$
$x = 30$	$q = -80$	$g = -40$
$n = 22$	$s = \frac{5}{12}$	

$\frac{1}{3}(27) - 4 = 5$

$9 - 4 = 5$

$5 = 5$

PAGE 90

$k = 5$	$w = -3$	$p = 20$
$t = 12$	$f = -18$	$u = 14$

PAGE 91

$w = 4.1$	$a = 7$	$y = 7\frac{1}{2}$
$c = -2.1$	$n = -14$	$v = -11$
$j = 18$	$g = 25.3$	$s = 5$

PAGE 92

$f = 7$	$w = -5$	$g = -\frac{3}{8}$
$t = 9$	$j = -7.5$	$y = \frac{2}{3}$
$n = -8$	$p = 10.2$	$d = 5\frac{7}{8}$

PAGE 93

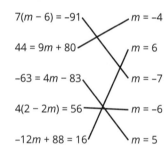

$7(m - 6) = -91$ → $m = -4$

$44 = 9m + 80$ → $m = 6$

$-63 = 4m - 83$ → $m = -7$

$4(2 - 2m) = 56$ → $m = -6$

$-12m + 88 = 16$ → $m = 5$

PAGE 94

$x = 5$	$x = 4$
$x = 17$	$x = -16$
$x = 6$	$x = 9$
$x = 96$	$x = 20$
$x = -10$	$x = -7$

DIVE-SION!

PAGE 95

$y = 8$	$g = 12$
$m = -4$	$a = -15$
$p = 2$	

PAGE 96

Equations may vary. Some possible equations are shown below.

$10t + 20 = 90$

$5p - 15 = 89$

$2n + 46 = 60$

PAGE 96, *continued*

4 (10.95 + *c*) = 55.60

1.25 (24 + *b*) = 83.75

PAGE 97

$14.99

$25

32 weeks

$\frac{1}{4}$ of a cup

PAGE 98

PAGE 99

$x \geq -1$	$x < 0$
$x > -5$	$x \leq 1$
$x \geq -\frac{1}{2}$	$x < -1.1$
$x > -\frac{3}{4}$	$x \leq -\frac{1}{10}$

PAGE 100

$x = 2$	$x = -4$
$x = 7$	$x = 3$
$y = -2$	$y = -11$
$y = 9$	$y = 9$
$z = 4$	$z = -1$
$z = 2$	$z = 5$

PAGE 100, *continued*

$m = -8$	$m = -2$
$m = -5$	$m = -3$
$t = 0$	$t = 6$
$t = 5$	$t = -6$
$q = -8$	$q = 8$
$q = 10$	$q = -2$
$r = -3$	$r = -5$
$r = -4$	$r = -1$
$p = 5$	$p = 10$
$p = -8$	$p = -10$

PAGE 101

$x > 5$

$m < 8$

$b > -5$

$a \geq 7$

$p \geq 4\frac{1}{2}$

$k < -1.6$

PAGE 102

$f < 5$

PAGE 102, *continued*

$g \geq 4$

$n > -3$

$d > -2$

$v > 1\frac{1}{2}$

PAGE 103

$q > -2$

$b < 3$

$f \geq -1.6$

$k \geq -1.7$

$u > -5$

$z > -4$

PAGE 103, *continued*

$n < -1\frac{1}{2}$

PAGE 104

Mandy's sister needs to grow at least 3 inches.

The second package should cost less than $11.75.

Ms. Popa needs to order at least 660 milliliters.

Fred should skate more than 12 laps.

PAGE 105

Ted wants to spend up to $60 on tennis supplies.

Mr. Dobbs will buy at least 27 books.

Maggie can buy no more than 2 pairs of shoes.

PAGE 106

$p \geq 1$

$r > -2$

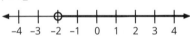

$g < -\frac{1}{2}$

$x \geq -8$

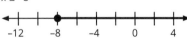

PAGE 107

$t \leq 14$

$b \geq 2.4$

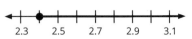

PAGE 107, *continued*

$x \leq -8$

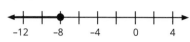

$h < 6$

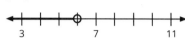

$r \geq 10$

PAGE 108

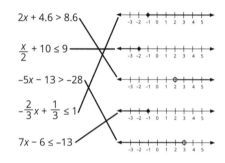

$2x + 4.6 > 8.6$

$\frac{x}{2} + 10 \leq 9$

$-5x - 13 > -28$

$-\frac{2}{3}x + \frac{1}{3} \leq 1$

$7x - 6 \leq -13$

PAGE 109

$s \leq 11$

$x < -2$

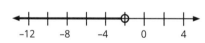

$n \geq 8$

$r < 16$

PAGE 109, *continued*

$v < 2$

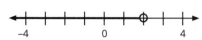

$w > 2.5$

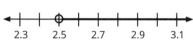

PAGE 110

Mr. Mobley can spend up to $7.20 on each gift.

Ada should practice at least $\frac{1}{3}$ of an hour each day.

Liam needs to save for more than 9 weeks.

Pete can buy at most 4 boxes of treats.

PAGE 111

Andre can give at most 4 cookies to each friend.

They can bring no more than 6 guests.

Lara can walk at least 10 dogs.

PAGE 112

all of the cars in the Northview Mall parking lot

all customers of Prized Pizza

all seventh grade students at Brooks Middle School

all graphic novels sold at Books for You chain of stores

all laptops for sale in the Best Tech stores

all people who work in Watertown

PAGE 113

No

No

Yes

Yes

No

PAGE 114

Answers will vary. Some possible answers are shown below.

Elizabeth could ask every fifth student who walks into the school in the morning.

PAGE 114, *continued*

Jayla could assign each ice cream shop a number. Then she could randomly choose 25 numbers and ask those ice cream shops.

Doug could put all of the words in a hat and randomly select 10 words. Then he could find the mean number of letters in the words that he chose.

Ms. Wade could assign each registered voter a number and randomly select 1% of those numbers.

The event manager could ask every 3rd soccer player who enters the soccer stadium.

PAGE 115

The population is every person in the world.

Answers will vary. Some possible answers are shown below.

I could collect data from everyone in my family. For one day, I will ask each person to record their heart rate in beats per minute at the start of every hour from 8 AM to 8 PM. I will then take all of the data and find the average heart rate. Since this average is in beats per minute, I will multiply that by 60 to find the average number of heartbeats per hour. Then, I will multiply that number by 24 to find the number of heartbeats per day.

This sample would not be a representative sample because it is not a random sample. It is not realistic for me to be able to collect data from people all over the world.

PAGE 116

30,000 yellow perch

PAGE 117

150 deer

40 cakes

42 students

PAGE 118

3	3	0	7
$7	$6.50	$5	$6
71	68	no mode	62
70	72.5	83	30

PAGE 119

2	1.6
6.4	8
3	6.5

PAGE 120

2

4

Answers will vary. One possible answer is shown below.

I agree with Terry's inference because the mean, or the average, is 2 pets per student.

73

15

Answers will vary. One possible answer is shown below.

I do not agree with Carlos's inference because the median is 73, which means half of the temperatures are above 73°F and half are below 73°F.

PAGE 121

Dance Depot

Rhythm Rhymes

Dance Depot

Dogs

Cats

Dogs

PAGE 122

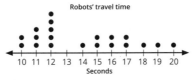

12

14

PAGE 123

Basketball

Basketball

Archery

Park

Movie theater

Park

PAGE 124

Time spent practicing last week

[box plot showing Hours from 0 to 10]

25%

6

PAGE 125

Planet Phone

Moon Mobile

Moon Mobile

Foxgloves

Sunflowers

Foxgloves

PAGE 126

$\frac{1}{4}$ or 25%

0 or 0%

$\frac{1}{2}$ or 50%

$\frac{3}{5}$ or 60%

$\frac{1}{5}$ or 20%

$\frac{4}{5}$ or 80%

PAGE 127

1 or 100%

0 or 0%

$\frac{1}{4}$ or 25%

$\frac{1}{5}$ or 20%

$\frac{2}{5}$ or 40%

0 or 0%

$\frac{4}{5}$ or 80%

$\frac{1}{10}$ or 10%

$\frac{3}{5}$ or 60%

Answers may vary. One possible answer is shown below.

In the last problem, a prime number is unlikely, while a number less than 1,000 is likely.

PAGE 128

P(3 or 7)	P(even number)	P(5)	P(> 2)	P(not a factor of 6)
P(not even)	P(multiple of 3)	P(not 6 or 7)	P(factor of 5)	P(> 8)
P(factor of 6)	P(≥ 9)	P(factor of 16)	P(0)	P(odd number)
P(less than 10)	P(not a multiple of 4)	P(> 3)	P(not < 5)	P(1)
P(not 4)	P(> 1)	P(not 2 or 3)	P(not 1)	P(multiple of 2)

PAGE 129

45 times
12 times
25 times

PAGE 130

$\frac{2}{5}$ or 40%

$\frac{3}{4}$ or 75%

$\frac{4}{5}$ or 80%

$\frac{1}{8}$ or 12.5%

PAGE 131

$\frac{1}{5}$ or 20%

$\frac{3}{10}$ or 30%

$\frac{1}{4}$ or 25%

PAGE 132

18 insects
25 customers
6 times

PAGE 133

4 times
5 people
20 fabric buttons

PAGE 134

not uniform
uniform
uniform
not uniform

PAGE 135

Models will vary. Some possible models are shown below.

Ethan

PAGE 136

Representation of sample space may vary. An organized list is shown below.
HG, TG, HB, TB, HR, TR, HO, TO
There are 8 possible outcomes.

PAGE 137

Representation of sample space may vary. Organized lists are shown below.
1H, 1T, 2H, 2T, 3H, 3T, 4H, 4T, 5H, 5T, 6H, 6T
There are 12 possible outcomes.

1A, 1B, 1C, 2A, 2B, 2C, 3A, 3B, 3C, 4A, 4B, 4C, 5A, 5B, 5C, 6A, 6B, 6C
There are 18 possible outcomes.

HHH, HHT, HTH, HTT, THH, THT, TTH, TTT
There are 8 possible outcomes.

PAGE 138

15 different combinations
9 different lunches
32 different combinations
48 different omelets

PAGE 139

$\frac{1}{4}$ or 25%

$\frac{1}{5}$ or 20%

PAGE 140

$\frac{1}{25}$ or 4%

$\frac{1}{5}$ or 20%

$\frac{1}{2}$ or 50%

$\frac{1}{4}$ or 25%

PAGE 141

$\frac{1}{5}$ or 20%

$\frac{3}{10}$ or 30%

PAGE 142

$\frac{1}{2}$ or 50%

Answers will vary. Some possible answers are shown below.
I could let the coin landing on heads represent a kitten having black fur and the coin landing on tails represent a kitten having brown fur.

For each trial, I would flip 4 coins to represent the 4 kittens.

PAGE 143

Answers will vary.

PAGE 144

independent
dependent
dependent
independent
dependent

PAGE 145

$\frac{1}{10}$ or 10%

$\frac{3}{20}$ or 15%

0 or 0%

PAGE 146

∠1
∠4 or ∠5
∠3

PAGE 147

∠2

∠4

∠1

∠2 or ∠5

∠1

∠4 and ∠6

∠2

∠6

∠2

PAGE 148

x = 17   h = 140

y = 58   d = 88

                t = 102

PAGE 149

f = 24   s = 8

p = 43   x = 7

g = 12   m = 41

PAGE 150

r = 15   v = 52

w = 196   p = 4

PAGE 151

48°

81°

57°

95°

76°

PAGE 152

b = 7   h = 15

r = 5   v = 15

g = 8   m = 11

PAGE 153

m∠1 = 135°   m∠2 = 45°   m∠3 = 135°

Answer may vary. One possible answer is shown below.

m∠6 = 45°

m∠6 = 45°

m∠4 = 135°   m∠5 = 45°   m∠7 = 135°

∠1, ∠3, ∠4, and ∠7 are congruent.

∠2, ∠5, ∠6, and the 45° angle are congruent.

PAGE 154

Yes   No   Yes

No   Yes   No

Yes   Yes   No

No   Yes   Yes

PAGE 155

k = 105°   b = 56°

x = 84°   p = 49.5°

y = 66°   g = 141.8°

PAGE 156

p = 23   n = 100

w = 29.5   f = 304

q = 33   t = 40

PAGE 157

Yes   Yes

No   No

Yes   No

No   Yes

PAGE 158

more than one triangle

one triangle

more than one triangle

no triangle

no triangle

more than one triangle

one triangle

more than one triangle

PAGE 159

20°

No

No

Answers will vary. Some possible answers are shown below.

11 millimeters

53 millimeters

PAGE 160

Polygons will vary. Some possible polygons are shown below.

PAGE 161

Polygons will vary. Some possible polygons are shown below.

PAGE 162

8 mi.   12 in.

38 yd.   16.5 ft.

              37 km

PAGE 163

Answers may vary. All answers are given using 3.14 as an approximation for π.

31.4 ft.   12.56 cm

94.2 in.   18.84 mi.

17.27 m   15.7 yd.

PAGE 164

Answers may vary. All answers are given using 3.14 as an approximation for π.

6.28 millimeters

31.4 yards

8 inches

PAGE 164, *continued*

7 kilometers

28.26 centimeters

6.5 meters

PAGE 165

Answers may vary. All answers are given using 3.14 as an approximation for π.

28.26 km^2 78.5 mm^2

50.24 in.^{2} 113.04 ft.^{2}

379.94 mi.^{2} 490.625 mm^2

PAGE 166

Answers may vary. All answers are given using 3.14 as an approximation for π.

153.86 square feet

12.56 square meters

200.96 square inches

38.465 square meters

572.265 square yards

PAGE 167

Answers may vary. All answers are given using 3.14 as an approximation for π.

113.04 square inches

37.68 meters

28.26 square meters

13 centimeters

7.536 feet

PAGE 168

Answers may vary. Some possible answers are shown below.

The areas of the two shapes are the same.

The areas of the two shapes are the same.

PAGE 169

circumference

Expression may vary. One possible expression is shown below.

$\frac{1}{2}(2\pi r)$

radius

r

PAGE 169, *continued*

Equation may vary. One possible equation is shown below.

Area = $\frac{1}{2}(2\pi r) \cdot r$

Area = πr^2

PAGE 170

56 cm^2 30 in.^{2}

35 ft.^{2} 31.5 mm^2

66.25 in.^{2}

PAGE 171

72 cm^2 138 in.^{2}

34 in.^{2} 42.25 yd.^{2}

9.9 cm^2

PAGE 172

Answers may vary. All answers are given using 3.14 as an approximation for π.

$A \approx$ 6.28 in.^{2} $A \approx$ 14.13 m^2

$P \approx$ 10.28 in. $P \approx$ 15.42 m

$A \approx$ 56.52 yd.^{2} $A \approx$ 76.93 cm^2

$P \approx$ 30.84 yd. $P \approx$ 35.98 cm

                          $A \approx$ 0.39 km^2

                          $P \approx$ 2.57 km

PAGE 173

75 mm^2 13.76 ft.^{2}

29.34 m^2 1.29 in.^{2}

PAGE 174

27 in.   54.84 mi.

73.12 mm   17.85 cm

88 in.   53.7 yd.

PAGE 175

30.84 mm   63.98 cm

10 ft. $42\frac{1}{2}$ in.

PAGE 176

24 in.^{2} 424 m^2

1,828 m^2 15 in.^{2}

342 mm^2 60.56 mm^2

PAGE 177

304.25 cm^2 443.75 mm^2

60 yd.^{2} 98.24 cm^2

PAGE 178

Scale factor = $\frac{1}{5}$

Scale factor = $\frac{5}{2}$

PAGE 179

$n = 4$ $x = 6$

$y = 3$

PAGE 180

Scaled copies may vary. Possible scaled copies are shown below.

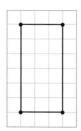

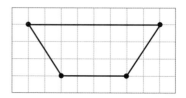

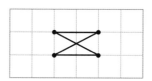

PAGE 181

Scaled copies may vary. Possible scaled copies are shown below.

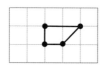

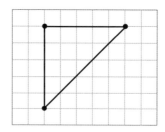

PAGE 182

1 inch : 3 kilometers

42 feet

1 inch : 0.5 meters

6 inches

$4\frac{1}{2}$ centimeters

PAGE 183

225 square inches
40 square centimeters
168 square feet
10 square feet
900 square inches

PAGE 184

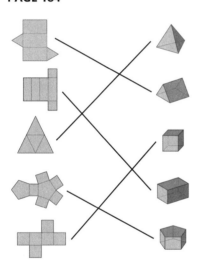

PAGE 185

166 ft.^{2} 54 in.^{2}

PAGE 186

424 in.^{2} 184 m^2
254 ft.^{2} 726 cm^2
                828 yd.^{2}

PAGE 187

$277\frac{1}{4}$ cm²   294.7 m²

40.56 ft.²   62.4 mm²

PAGE 188

156 cm²   25.7 in.²

PAGE 189

12.9 yd.^{2} 88 in.^{2}
83.25 ft.^{2} 55 cm^2
270 ft.^{2}

PAGE 190

596 m^2 323 in.^{2}
416 yd.^{2} 384 cm^2

PAGE 191

65 square feet
82 square inches
152 square feet
781.25 square centimeters

PAGE 192

180 in.^{3} 560 mm^3
216 cm^3 567 yd.^{3}

PAGE 193

1.728 mm^3 234 in.^{3}
3 cm   5 ft.
4 m

PAGE 194

96 ft.^{3} 324 m^3

10 cm^3 $3\frac{1}{3}$ yd^3

PAGE 195

26 cm^3 $\frac{1}{4}$ ft.^{3}

1,302 mm^3 19.2 ft.^{3}

$\frac{3}{4}$ m^3

PAGE 196

$4\frac{1}{8}$ mm^3 300 in.^{3}

130 ft.^{3} 472 cm^3

                72 in.^{3}

PAGE 197

3,375 cubic inches
8 cubic meters
Cube container
4.8 yards

PAGE 198

PAGE 199

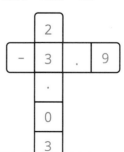

PAGE 200

12.3	–14	42
$-\frac{2}{27}$	$\frac{1}{4}$	$-\frac{3}{25}$
$\frac{1}{5}$	40	–1.4
$-8\frac{4}{5}$	$\frac{6}{11}$	$-25\frac{7}{8}$

Answers may vary. All answers are provided in decimal form.

6.8   9.9   –4.275

PAGE 201

19.25 − (−3.78) = 23.03
−15.16 + 11.26 = −3.9

PAGE 201, *continued*

$57 + (-6.02) = 50.98$

$-9.4 \times (-5.3) = 49.82$

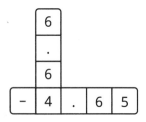

$-18.6 \div 4 = -4.65$

$-83 \div (-12.5) = 6.64$

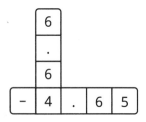

$-8.1 \times (-2.9) = 23.49$

$-16.7 - 17.4 = -34.1$

PAGE 202

$x = 3$	$a = 9$	$h = -5$
$k = 1$	$m = -3$	$p = 6$
$n = 0.5$	$b = -\frac{1}{4}$	$c = 4$
$v = -20$	$z = \frac{3}{8}$	$r = 16$

PAGE 203

$25

4 revolutions

$29.10

$7.50

PAGE 204

7/20 or 35%

1/20 or 5%

8 times

6 balls

7/25 or 28%

PAGE 205

Representations of sample spaces may vary. An organized list is shown below.

H1, T1, H2, T2, H3, T3, H4, T4, H5, T5

There are 10 possible outcomes in the sample space.

3/10 or 30%

2/10 or 20%

1/10 or 10%

PAGE 206

$k = 2$ $k = 7$

$k = 5$ $k = \frac{1}{3}$

$k = \frac{3}{5}$ $k = 0.59$

PAGE 207

No

Yes

Yes

PAGE 208

Number of clues	Number of coins
2	6
4	12
8	24
16	48

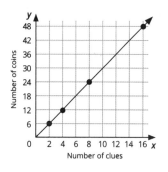

PAGE 208, *continued*

$y = 3x$

(1, 3)

This point means when Benny finds 1 clue, he earns 3 coins.

(12, 36)

This point means when Benny finds 12 clues, he earns 36 coins.

PAGE 209

Number of stickers	Cost ($)
2	3
4	6
6	9
8	12

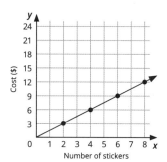

$y = 1.5x$

$1.50

(1, 1.5)

$4.50

(3, 4.5)